A WILDERNESS OF DAYS

A
WILDERNESS
OF
DAYS

An artist's experiences as a prisoner of war in Germany

MAXWELL BATES

1978

SONO NIS PRESS
1745 Blanshard Street, Victoria, British Columbia, Canada

Canadian Cataloguing in Publication Data

Bates, Maxwell, 1906-
    A wilderness of days

    ISBN 0-919462-56-1

      1. World war, 1939-1945 — Prisoners and prisons,
German. 2. World war, 1939-1945 — Personal
narratives, Canadian. 3. Bates, Maxwell, 1906-
I. Title.

D805.G3B38   940.54'72'43   C78-002015-4

Published by
SONO NIS PRESS
1745 Blanshard Street, Victoria, B.C.

Designed and printed in Canada by
MORRISS PRINTING COMPANY LTD.
Victoria, British Columbia

TO
Charlotte

CONTENTS

PREFACE

The march of Allied prisoners of war into Holland in June 1940, and the longer march in Germany in 1945 were minor historical events caused by two enormous upheavals — the fall of France and the fall of Germany.

Throughout *Gefangenschaft* the march of 1940 was always called "the March" by the British prisoners of war who took part in it. It was an ever recurring subject of conversation (second, perhaps, only to women) from the summer of 1940 until the march of 1945.

In writing of the period between marches, for me five years, it would be misleading to describe merely the light and dark events — most of the picture should be in middle tones. There was endless repetition and routine. This, of course, applies to life in general. I have tried to convey something of the reality, as it appeared to me.

THE MARCH, 1940

I

The March began in the early afternoon of June 12th. I was a private in a machine-gun battalion of the Middlesex Regiment, itself attached to the 51st Highland Division. For the purposes of the campaign this Division was part of the French IX Corps under General Ihler. We stood, under the guns of German tanks, in long, irregular lines on a hillside two or three miles inland from St. Valéry-en-Caux. I had heard no talk of surrender. Rather, we had retained some hope that, at the last moment, we should find a way out.

During the previous twenty-four hours I could have made off alone, or with a companion, and attempted to reach unoccupied country to the south. But deserter is an ugly word. Besides, we understood the Germans were on three sides of us; the fourth side, north-west, was the English Channel. It was a question how much sea-coast was occupied. But the idea of escape was at the back of my mind. A persistent and welcome rumour that we would form a fighting spearhead to the sea helped to forestall such an attempt. The intention was to capture the German held cliffs overlooking St. Valéry harbour to allow the evacuation by sea. Unfortunately French troops surrendering at intervals between the Germans and the British prevented the attack. Any action was better than waiting in the drizzling rain. I gave up a chance to get away (it came up before the idea had occurred to me) at noon on the 11th. My Company Sergeant Major, Quartermaster Sergeant and a driver took a truck; they asked me if I wanted to go with them. After the war I learned that they drove south to Fécamp without mishap and reached England.

Before surrender our junior officers had little accurate knowledge of the military position. Information about the Dunkirk evacuation, completed some eight days previously, had not reached the ranks. A few days before, after the Dunkirk evacuation, the Division had attacked the German held bridgehead at Abbeville on the Somme. As our barrage began at three in the morning there was a general impression, at our advanced Company Headquarters, that the operation would be successful. But the Division suffered heavy losses and the Germans held the bridgehead.

Northern France was disorganized. We disregarded the pessimistic news from French soldiers. But French opinion was comparatively accurate and our faith was based on success in other wars; we were irritated by *trés difficile*, shrugged shoulders, and a description of how the Germans would attempt to invade England. Though we knew that German quicksilver tank movements were cutting the Division off, and a French division or two, it wasn't generally accepted in our ranks that the Battle of France was lost. But we all knew the campaign was going badly during a series of withdrawals. German planes bombed and machine-gunned us daily. We had no air support. So the 51st, a great Division, reached the vicinity of St. Valéry depleted by 10,000 casualties. After the Dunkirk evacuation there were still about 140,000 British troops in France. The 51st was attempting to reach Le Havre to be evacuated.

D Company, to which I belonged, occupied a dozen towns and villages during the period of withdrawal. During the most peaceful hours, such as a day in the inland village of St. Maxent billeted in an evacuated cottage among half-open drawers, torn letters, old petticoats, a fly buzzing in the window; watching the leisurely movements of a cow in the sunny pasture (she was milked by a soldier) there was edginess caused by extreme boredom and a sense of approaching disaster.

On June 11th we expected to see ships at St. Valéry but by the morning of the 12th we knew there were no ships to transport the Division to England.

Our prospects kept changing on the 11th. Before noon, as our trucks approached St. Valéry, we met several British soldiers who warned us that the road into St. Valéry was being shelled, and that we were cut off. Where they were marching, I don't know, for the road lead to Veules-les-Roses, a village we had left hurriedly an hour before because we expected German tanks. Our Company Commander decided without hesitation to drive on to St. Valéry. I rode in the back of a large supply truck, sitting high up on cases of machine-gun ammunition and grenades. The column stopped at a fork in the road. We heard machine-gun and rifle fire beyond a wooded hill rising steeply from the fork. The Company set up machine guns in concealed positions some distance from the road. With three others I was ordered to lie in the fork to fire at German tanks if they approached us. We only had rifles and would be lucky to break a steel link of the caterpillars.

Several small detachments of French infantry straggled past. They were going into the line or, more often, coming out. A giant Frenchman leading a white horse harnessed to an anti-tank gun refused to stay with us.

Nothing happened for five or six hours. Once I left the road to help carry ammunition up the steep slope to the troops carrying on the "battle" at the top. It took a long time for two of us to carry and drag the heavy wooden box by its rope handles up through trees, roots and thick bushes. We carried it a mile: the troops were not so close as we expected. They were the weary survivors of several battalions occupying a long line.

We remained at the fork until dark. Then the Company trucks moved forward on the St. Valéry road. The column stopped about two miles from the town. Essential parts of truck engines were thrown away. Divisional Artillery, who had joined us, damaged their guns and abandoned them. Leaving the trucks parked at the roadside we marched in darkness, carrying only bren guns, machine guns, ammunition boxes and rifles. Most of our kit was left in the trucks. Machine guns and ammunition were heavy enough to carry and our kit bags would overload the boats.

A red glow showed St. Valéry's position; parts of the town were on fire. We reached the outskirts and passed a railway signal tower bursting into flame. Piles of ammunition nearby popped and spluttered like fire-crackers. The road was lit up and, as there might be German snipers, we dashed across glaring patches of light into the darkness beyond. I carried a brass machine-gun tripod, but those who carried machine-gun ammunition — a wooden box between two men — had a heavier and clumsier burden. A machine gun (German we thought) fired intermittent bursts from the south side of the town as we marched through cobblestone streets between the uninterrupted walls of houses. The moon had risen; the houses seemed deserted. We halted near the market place and waited for several hours in ranks of five. Sergeants gave detailed embarkation orders. The ranks became cheerful. We heard rumours of all kinds and by eleven o'clock the delay seemed to be caused by German control of the beach with machine guns. We heard there were many casualties. At last we realized there were no ships, except one destroyer lying seven miles out. Long afterwards it became known that one of our officers swam out to the destroyer, found that the fog had prevented naval forces from arriving, and swam back to report to Divisional Headquarters, unhurt although fired at while crossing the beach. There was no reliable information at the time.

Many wounded British soldiers lay on stretchers, and a larger number of French wounded lay in the streets and in the houses.

Between one and two in the morning the ranks began to break up. Sergeants told the men to spend the night in an orchard on a hillside north of the town. Many began to drift in that direction, but nothing was definite: definite orders had ceased.

With a friend, also in D Company, I entered the open doorway of a house. We preferred to sleep under a roof; rain had begun to fall during the hours of waiting. There were sounds of heavy breathing. The flame of my friend's match revealed bandaged, sleeping men. They covered the floor, but there was enough space for him to lie near the doorway and I, with difficulty, reached a narrow strip of table at the end of the room. It was easy to sleep; we had so little time for it. Even so, I was awakened by explosions and bursts of machine-gun and rifle fire. Wounded men groaned and cried out during the night.

It was still raining in the early morning, but it was quieter. The machine guns still fired a few rounds now and then in the south side of the town. They were German posts on the cliffs overlooking the harbour, but we didn't know that.

For some time we searched for British troops; our companions of the night were French. About five-thirty we found some of our men who had spent a wet night in the orchard, and we all walked the two miles back to the abandoned trucks. Most of the Company was there. Several Indian Army reservists had taken possession of the truck where I had left my kit bag, my greatcoat and some chocolate. When I attempted to climb up for them I was threatened with bayonets. A sergeant ordered them to give me my things. He was told what he could do with himself. These reservists, who had served their seven years in the British Army in India, were put into a Territorial Regiment to stiffen it before it became part of the Middlesex Regiment — their presence was detrimental, in my opinion, in spite of the good men among them. We stood in the rain, waiting. I thought I had got into a nasty pocket of space and time; that is how I described it to myself.

The morning hours were quiet except for the sound of an occasional bullet. A woman left behind when the town was evacuated, the only civilian I had seen for two or three days, stood in the road talking to some French soldiers. One of our officers arrived and ordered a machine gun to be set up. The number one on the gun (the man who fires it), an Indian Army Reservist, wore a red bandanna handkerchief round his neck. It wouldn't have been tolerated before that morning. Some men stretched out in the ditch to sleep in the rain. I watched the massive hill rising parallel to the road with a cemetery near its top. Hundreds of tombstones would give good cover to an advancing enemy. The only farmhouse visible was the Divisional Headquarters about three-quarters of a mile away.

About noon several mortar shells whistled overhead. Then a bugle at Divisional Headquarters sounded the "Cease Fire".

One of our officers ordered us to throw away rifles, bayonets and ammunition. No Germans were in sight. We were incredulous, then angry and disgusted. We still hoped to make a foray to the sea. We snapped our bayonets in two; threw the bolts of our rifles in bushes and tall grass; cast our cartridges on the ground, and walked across the road to a field on the side of a hill. Tanks arrived suddenly. The Germans standing on them held long barrelled pistols; unlike the British and French they were not wearing steel helmets. We waited for orders and tore up papers which might be useful to the enemy. Many tore up French hundred franc banknotes, their army pay. I destroyed sketches and notes but I kept my money: fifteen 100 franc notes.

We filed out from the north corner of the field; crossed the road and climbed the long slope of the hill. I saw General Fortune sitting on a large stone beside the road. This Commander of the 51st Highland Division, greatly respected, later refused repatriation although a sick man, until every one of his Division was released. Later I passed General Rommel, the German Commander, although I did not know who he was at the time.

II

In single file we climbed the deeply rutted path to the northern ridge: an irregular line of khaki figures ending at the skyline.

A greatcoat lay on the grass, dropped by someone already tired by the climb. For several months I regretted leaving it there. Higher up, I picked up an army haversack. It was lighter than the greatcoat and had a shaving kit inside. I used both for five years. I felt better, having something useful that belonged to me besides my uniform and gas cape. I had kept the gas cape to keep off the rain. It was like green oilskin; weighed practically nothing; and was provided as a protection from liquid gas. My gas mask and water bottle had been abandoned when we left our trucks.

The flat, high land north of the valley gave a long view of wheat-fields stretching to majestic banks of cumulus cloud. The scattered column slowly made its way to the east, passing, now and then, a German soldier. One of them took a pair of fur gloves my companion had tucked in his belt. German tanks had flattened the wheat in a straight line and we marched in this road. After three or four hours a donkey joined us and ambled beside us carrying my companion's greatcoat and kit on his back.

We were hungry and thirsty. Since breakfast the day before we had eaten only raisins and chocolate.

The afternoon was fine after the morning rain, even hot, so that as the column reached several farmhouses, after crossing the horizon-bounded fields, we rushed to a hand pump. Here, every man showed a preoccupation with his own needs and a disregard for others that characterized the march. French and British soldiers struggled for water in a way that prevented most of them from getting any, so much of the precious liquid, sparkling in the sun, was spilled by jostling and pushing. Guards shouted and threatened. I begged a cup of milk from an old peasant woman at the back door of a cottage while the guards broke up the crowd round the pump.

From now on, continual vigilance was needed to survive. No opportunity could be lost to obtain food and drink.

We marched as if on an interminable road in a dream.

A group of German Air Force officers stood in front of a farmhouse. They came out to watch us pass by in the late afternoon quiet. "For you the war is over," one of them called out in English. All British prisoners of war heard these words again and again in 1940. In June 1940, many Germans believed that the war would be over for them, too, in ten days.

About 6:30 that evening we marched downhill into a town and waited a long time on a grass verge near the road. The general opinion was that we would rest in the town for the night. Cars passed rapidly taking officers of high rank on business of the German Army, or their own. A fat officer wearing an eye-glass, each arm round a pretty girl, flashed past in the back of an open car. It was like a scene in a Hollywood film. He and the prisoners illustrated the sudden and unexpected inequalities of war.

We entered a farmyard and passed a wedge of fifty or sixty British officers seated on the grass. From the beginning our officers were separated from us. We passed a pond and a mass of men struggling at the farm pump, and went on to an orchard at the end of the farmyard because every foot of ground was occupied. The orchard was more pleasant; there was grass and it was only sparsely populated.

We made our way to the pump. We needed water badly but few British prisoners had water bottles. The French were so numerous, had so many water bottles, and were so single-minded in their pursuit of water that it was difficult to get a drink. The pump was the scene of continual quarrelling, shouting and shoving. Neither British nor French formed queues. Every man was on his own. I realized my complete unimportance in the eyes of everyone else.

From the orchard we watched a haystack being demolished for bedding. Undermined, it caved in and engulfed several gesticulating figures. We settled down on the comfortable grass. My friend had a tin of herrings and, with the prospect of a night's rest before us, we felt more cheerful. "Some day you can stand me a dinner in London," he said.

Shouting "Raus mit! Los!" German guards ran into the orchard. We were rounded up and driven out. Another large batch of prisoners was coming to the farmyard. To make room for them we had to go farther up the road, but not much farther. No one near us understood German but that is what we thought they told us.

It was still twilight. We left the farm with regret for we were very weary. We reached the outskirts of the town and passed the last scattered houses without any sign of stopping.

"Los! Los!" The guards quickened the pace. Shots were fired over our heads. All along the line guards shouted, and the column of five abreast broke into a fast walk. The pace was sporadic. The guards were not satisfied and fired again. The men were too tired and began to cast off greatcoats and haversacks. As the threats ceased we slowed down. Then the shouting and rifle shots began again and the column trotted another hundred yards.

The moon had risen. We passed along country lanes between shadowy trees.

The jogging pace dislodged things from the haversacks of men in front. Several "fifty" boxes of Woodbine cigarettes fell on the road, but although I badly needed cigarettes, I was too exhausted to pick them up. So was everyone else. Every man settled down to gazing vacantly at the back of the man ahead.

During four or five hours we crossed moonlit landscape. At last we reached a farmyard similar to the one we had left, and stood in the road for a long time. Two or three men near me collapsed. I fell forward on my face but regained consciousness quickly and moved forward into the farmyard with the others. I found a few vacant feet of gravel path but had hardly enough strength to spread my gas cape as a ground sheet.

We remained in the farmyard the next day and night and, at the muddy edge of its stagnant pond, I washed and shaved. The farm pump was the scene of a day-long struggle for water with repeated but unsuccessful attempts to form a queue system. To wait patiently was to go without.

About noon, a Captain in my Company found several of us who were D-Company men and gave us a quantity of canned food. For this purpose he had carried it in his haversack. He was billeted in one of the barns with other officers and was the last British officer I saw for two years.

The Germans collected steel helmets and gas masks from those who still carried them. They asked for all razors and knives but no one gave up anything useful that could be kept out of sight. Very few British had an army cap with them, and many kept the wire contraption fixed in steel helmets. This wire gave no protection from the sun or the weather yet hundreds wore it. Most of the French had their pointed army caps or berets. They had food and clothing with them, and seemed to have been prepared to surrender.

Men who were lucky found a piece of grass to lie on for the night, instead of mud or stony earth. Those with greatcoats had a better chance to sleep: the night was clear and cold.

Soon after sunrise we were packed into several large trucks in a standing position. All day we drove through many more or less damaged towns, among them Yvetot which I remembered, having been there before. We had turned south on a circuitous route; the reason for which escaped us. We unloaded in a large field commanded from one corner by a machine gun mounted on a wooden tower. The field was marshy. To keep fires alight was difficult, but the ingenuity of prisoners of war is unlimited, and smoke rose from a score of fires in a few minutes. Night had not yet fallen, so brisk trading between French and British troops began and continued until after dark. One of the French soldiers I approached answered my broken French in English. He had nothing. He was an American who had joined the French Army in 1939. We slept in water. As the night wore slowly on, it began to rain heavily.

Before going to sleep a British prisoner who lay near me put his boots under his head as a pillow. During the night they were carefully extracted and stolen. I removed my boots at night to ease my feet, but I was careful to tie the lace ends to my belt and to arrange the boots in a safe position.

It was foolhardy to leave anything unguarded at any time, so we began to form groups. One man always stayed to keep a place selected for sleeping; or to guard belongings while the others washed in a stream, or tried to exchange some article for food. Later, in Germany, these groups became known as combines or syndicates and shared Red Cross parcels issued to the members. While on the march, a group stood alone and could rely only on itself. A member of a group shared anything he acquired.

Food was more important than anything else. We talked about food. We imagined lavish feasts, and these fantasies lessened the boredom and fatigue of marching. Freud, in his *Introductory Lectures on Psychoanalysis*, tells about a group of Arctic explorers who recorded in their journal the prevalence of food dreams while undergoing a period of hunger. We, also, when able to sleep in spite of the cold, dreamed of food in infinite variety, just as, months and years later, a dream of leave or a visit home was often mentioned.

We ended our march at a field or orchard in the late afternoon. More or less exhausted, we lit a fire between two stones if, some time during the day, we had grubbed a few potatoes out of the ground while the guards were occupied or looking elsewhere. Sometimes we boiled plantains and dandelion leaves. Our official rations were pitiful. Soon after sunrise we lined up with tin cans or mess tins for coffee water made from burnt grain or acorns. Few British prisoners had army mess tins. More common was a battered tin cup or rusty tin can picked up on the march.

On a few occasions two or three hard tack biscuits, British rations fallen to the enemy, were handed out and for these we waited a long time in queues. These queues were orderly because the Germans intended to prevent any man getting two rations. In the evening, after marching about thirty-five kilometres, a ladle of beans and water was spilled into our cans. Fortunately the French people in the towns and villages we passed through were generous and came out of their houses with bread, milk and sometimes cider. But there were too many of us for one man to obtain enough. For several days thousands had passed through so that, although the French people were surprisingly willing to give, they hadn't much to spare.

We spent several days in this way, passing through towns, some of the buildings flattened except for brick chimneys standing above the ruins.

On the sixth day, as we reached a small town at noon, the guards tightened discipline. Before, there had only been shouted threats or a rifle shot when men rushed to a pump for water; or someone ran for a piece of bread brought to door or window by a civilian. Things I had done often. But, as we entered this town, soldiers opened up with automatic rifles on several men running across the road to collect bread. Five or six fell; shot in the legs. A man just behind me was shot dead for leaving the column to pluck a handful of onions. We were forced to run until we were outside the town, a terrible effort in our weak condition.

Next day, June 18th, we reached two large fields near Doumont. The fields, sloping up the side of a hill, were over-crowded with several thousand men. The grass had become hard-packed earth. Only a limited number were sent on each morning, and I contrived to stay three days. In the daytime the hillside was too hot, at night bitterly cold. It was better than marching. My friend and I joined others to make a group of seven or eight, all of the same regiment, before we left Doumont. One had dashed into a deserted house as we marched through a town and found a large lace curtain, slightly better than nothing when laid over three or four of us. Someone had an army groundsheet. Laid sideways it protected three men from the cold ground. But we slept little; chattering teeth and numb feet made it difficult.

The French prisoners called to each other continually. Cries of "André", "Marcel", etc. were incessant until darkness had long fallen on the hillside. Calling their comrades was a characteristic of the French. They were separated during the day, because some men walked quickly to reach the front of the column for a better chance to get food from civilians. Others, weary and with sore feet, fell more and more behind, although the Germans tried to keep us five abreast in some order. The long drawn-out cries got on our nerves.

The peremptory and furious demand: "taisez-vous," of those British who knew some French, no doubt frayed French nerves.

At Doumont I read Virginia Wolfe's *The Common Reader* twice, and I read it again before it was confiscated in Germany. It was in my inside battledress pocket when I was captured — a paperback edition. I had also a French vocabulary, a mere pamphlet. One of our group had a French farmers' guide or almanac that he had picked up in a farmhouse before capture. That was the extent of our library until a Scotsman gave me his New Testament to lesson the weight he had to carry.

A pocket New Testament weighs only a few ounces but it made a difference. No day went by without thought on my part about how to carry less. I don't know how I could have carried a greatcoat although I needed one so much at night. An endless debate with myself concerned a wine bottle I had picked up. It hung from my shoulder by an army rifle pull-through cord. Some means of carrying water was necessary, but I doubted whether the pain in my shoulder caused by its weight was worth the precious water. I took the New Testament, knowing it would be invaluable in the future, but in due course it was confiscated.

The column took on a raffish look after several nights in fields, and days marching on dusty roads. Most prisoners were without razors or soap and had the beginnings of beards. Headgear was queer from the start. The inside wire framework of steel helmets was to be seen on half the British heads. A few old felt and slouch hats appeared. Some wore a khaki handkerchief knotted at the corners and others, like myself, used an inside battledress jacket pocket that looked like an army cap. Several coloured bedspreads and curtains had been stolen and were wound round the waists of their new owners, or slung over their shoulders. Many French wore their pale blue army greatcoats and, here and there, a French North African soldier had the large red cap called a Tarboosh. The endless procession was strangely unmilitary and piratical in character. There were, on the other hand, British soldiers who looked almost smart to the end.

The column seemed endless. Where the road could be seen far ahead the front of the column was out of sight. All resting places had

been in use for two weeks. Of course, the vast majority of prisoners was French.

We frequently passed wooden signs nailed to posts at the side of the road, with the printed words *Bahn* or *Lager* and an arrow. An inadequate knowledge of German (the confusion of *Bahn* with *Eisenbahn*) lead to the idea that we were marching to a railway junction and the old train rumour revived. From the first there was a rumour that we would be transported by train.

Next to food and drink the most persistent thought was how to let people at home know we were alive. We suspected that we should be posted as "missing," which in fact happened. Several times the Red Cross gave us food. It must have been arranged with the German authorities because on these occasions we were halted and ordered to sit in rows in a field. Nurses arrived in a truck (I think they were French) and distributed a sandwich to every man. At the same time slips of paper were collected with the names and addresses of next-of-kin. Of course I took advantage of this service, but none of the notes reached home.

The idea of escaping was in all our minds at different times, and it is strange that so few made the attempt during the march. The fact that we were not permitted by International Law to escape at this stage deterred no one. This was the best time to escape. I think the physical and mental state at the time of capture, and the hard life that followed, left no energy for escape. I often missed the opportunity of getting a piece of bread offered by a civilian by my sheer inability to make the extra effort to reach it before someone else: my weakness from lack of food prevented me from getting it under conditions of extreme competition. I found it hard enough to keep in the ranks, making up my mind to reach some landmark and when that was reached setting a new objective. But I must not give the impression that the column was dispirited. Nothing of the kind. Irritability was common and perhaps none of us was far from anger on any provocation. Everyone was depressed at times, then and later, but few showed it.

I think I was most depressed at Doullens. At sunset, on the evening of the 21st of June, we turned off the main road and entered an old prison fort. It was not a building, although we passed buildings at

25

its entrance on our way in. It was an area of trees, bushes, rocks and large bare patches of ground contained on three sides by stone walls at least one hundred feet high. The walls had been built to enclose a hill. I stood at the top of the wall made of huge pieces of gray stone, before guards were posted to prevent us reaching it, and saw a tremendous view of the countryside. I imagined that the place had been a stronghold in the Middle Ages. Inside, the ground sloped roughly down from the top of the walls to form a bowl. Our group stayed in this hellish place two days. During the day it was very hot for the sides of the bowl seemed to hold and intensify the sunlight. It was overcrowded and rations were ridiculously meagre. Tempers rose. It rained for several hours each night.

A large marquee gave cover to two hundred, only a fraction of the teeming mass of prisoners. When rain began to fall I managed to get inside but, prevented by overcrowding from lying down, I remained jammed unable to move arms or legs all night. A comical situation developed when men on both sides of me threatened to fight me in the morning because I tried to shift my legs. I understood the meaning of claustrophobia.

At Doullens the German Kommandant threatened severe disciplinary action because some men took double rations. The guards made us form up in ranks while he gave a speech interpreted by a French prisoner. The gist of it was that enough soup had been provided to allow each man a ladleful. A number of men must have got into the queue twice because there were about fifty men without soup. Unless the men who had taken two rations confessed he would not issue any more food. These men who had robbed their comrades must step out of the ranks and form up separately. Of course, no one moved. The Kommandant, in a furious temper, announced that no more rations would be issued until the offenders confessed. In due course, however, rations were issued, such as they were.

There was a German military doctor at Doullens. Anyone with a serious disability he could show received attention. One of our group reported sick and brought us cans of peas and sardines bought from a French orderly employed by the Germans.

It is fair to say that those with very bad feet or some other obvious disability were transported in limited numbers by truck. But many men began to suffer from dysentry, most inconvenient on the march. Sometimes these unfortunates received the butt end of a rifle for leaving the column to obey the calls of nature. Dysentry was common among prisoners of war for many months. But the German medical treatment of British prisoners of war was adequate in most cases, and better than their treatment in any other respect.

A characteristic feature of the march was the rough handling of civilians offering food on the road. Usually the givers were women, and sometimes children sent into the road by their mothers with a handful of bread or a jug of cider. Often a dozen men closed swiftly upon a friendly woman and, in the struggle to seize something before the next man could get it, she was mauled. I saw white haired women knocked flat on their backs, others with torn clothing and many frightened and upset. Occasionally an arm or a leg was broken. One was likely to see, when a scrimmage had cleared, the broken pieces of a milk jug and a child in tears. Proportionately not many were responsible for this violence, but enough to ensure something of the sort in whichever part of the column I happened to be. Others never left the ranks for any reason. I got a good deal of bread from civilians and wonder how I could have kept going without it. It was unnecessary to maul anyone. Unfortunately men tried to knock bread out of the hands of others receiving it. Only the guards' rifles prevented the column from becoming a continuous free fight.

The defeat of France, and England's danger in consequence, were not apprehended at anything like their true value. It would be an exaggeration to say we were not concerned about it, but we did not think about it often. Thoughts were personal and concerned with things at hand: physical discomfort confined thought to the moment and the place, and the period immediately preceding capture was much the same. The significance of what lay before our eyes during the Battle of France was lost in the effort to escape dive-bombing, hedge-hopping planes while rapidly moving from a village about to be taken to another which would be threatened in its turn the following night (sometimes we left a village at one end as German tanks entered at the other); in an effort to obtain cheap champagne and a large variety of liqueurs, in the difficulties, discomforts and

annoyances of one's particular duty. Our minds were occupied with trivia.

On June 23rd the march for the day ended at a race track outside the town of St. Pol. There had been a widely credited rumour that our march would end there. We would board a train at St. Pol, known to be a railway junction by men billeted there during the winter of '39 to '40. There was great disappointment when the prediction proved to be false.

On this day while crossing a wide plain and passing through several small, grim towns we heard of the fall of France. A vendor offered the first Nazi propaganda newspaper printed in French that we had seen. A French woman warned us of them. "Est-ce allemand?" "Oui, oui, pas bon!"

At St. Pol, for the first time, we received an inch square piece of meat with our beans. Some of us traded with civilians at the edge of the road that bounded the race track on one side. It happened that the hand pump where we washed was near the road, and by crawling through tall grass it was possible to talk to people in the road and exchange things through the wire fence without being seen. But it meant a long wait with the probability of failure, for the guards kept an eye on passing civilians. Among ourselves there was a considerable trade. French soldiers gave biscuits and chocolates for watches, fountain pens and knives. A few sheets of rusty galvanized-iron bent in a semi-circular shape gave cover for the night to those who secured a place under them. Most, as usual, slept under the sky.

What followed was for many of us the memorable day of the march. Between St. Pol and Béthune the French people turned out along the road with food and drink. Sandwiches, cake, milk, cider, were distributed in quantities. We marched as usual for the first few miles. Then civilians began to appear at doors and the entrances to lanes. I received a towel and soap from a nun and everyone must have received some necessary article. British and French were treated alike. The guards were not so strict, no doubt because the official rations were obviously insufficient, and the latter part of the afternoon was more like a triumphant procession than a march into captivity. At Béthune a large crowd of civilians watched us march through the market place. A frantic woman kept repeating an

29

English name. We went into the sports ground and were given better rations than any we had so far received: pea soup with some horse meat. There was bombing at a considerable distance, a sound we found encouraging. During the night it rained. Rain, until later when we were often sheltered in an empty building, was our enemy as much as the Germans, at its worst during the cold nights. At dawn, some of us tried to shelter on the tiers of concrete seats of the roofed over grandstand. Space was hard to find. The attempt lead to bad temper and abusive language from disturbed recumbent figures.

We reached Seclin on the evening of the 25th and my group claimed a patch of school playground as a place to sleep. There was trading with the inhabitants, in spite of the guards, over a brick wall. It required a trusting nature because the only way was to toss money, or whatever one wanted to trade with, over the wall. In due course a packet of Elegante or Gaulois cigarettes fell on the grass beside us. I bought four packets in this way, which says much for the honesty of the inhabitants. Those who waited two hours in a queue received half a cup of wine from the Germans. My group preferred to rest on the grass.

The following day we reached the Belgian border. The houses were cleaner and better than any we had seen in northern France. We occasionally received bread from the people, but not enough to give us strength. I began to read my French vocabulary while marching; memorizing a dozen words and repeating them to myself without looking at the page.

The days were hot and I drank water as often as I could get it, although it is unwise to drink much while marching. I remember the rotten-cider taste of the pump water, not unpleasant at the time, and its yellow colour.

We reached the pleasant Belgian town of Tournai on the 26th and were quartered in a huge barracks. After lining up for rations in the courtyard and washing, it was discovered that food could be bought through a small hole in a brick wall near the latrines. By placing a few sentries to give warning of guards, food and cigarettes were bought from Belgian children. Indian native troops with turbans squatted forlornly near the latrines. Later, a French soldier in the courtyard gave me a bar of chocolate and would accept nothing for it. Regarded in its true relation to the times, and the special values then current (he could have got a gold watch for it) it was an instance of remarkable generosity.

A disused flax textile factory at Ninove sheltered us on the next night, and on the following night, a stage farther on, I slept under an apple tree in an orchard adjoining a factory. An Englishman I met for the first time here offered me a job after the war. There was a canteen stall with lemonade for sale, but very little could be bought at these canteens set up by enterprising civilians. The supply was exhausted by the first hundred men to arrive. Here and there on the road a civilian on a bicycle would suddenly dismount, where he was not seen by guards for a moment, and dispose of packets of tobacco at a great profit. When crowding through a town it was sometimes possible to enter a shop unobserved and to make a quick purchase. Usually the shopkeepers were willing to sell, but the guards watched for such attempts and there was seldom enough time. I bought two pairs of socks and some food at different times. At a favourable moment a gang left the column to strip a vegetable garden. A swarm of locusts would not do more damage. The gardens belonged to people who helped us voluntarily as much as possible. But ethical considerations tended to recede to the fringes of the mind. I was forced to regret such a foray by indigestion. The position of a barn containing a pile of raw sugar beet allowed a stream of men to enter and leave unobserved. The pile disappeared in a few minutes and most of the beets were eaten on the spot (the beets would have to be hidden from guards). While marching I ate rhubarb when I found it, and could pluck it from the side of the road, sucking the sticks for many weary miles.

We reached Aalst on the 29th and entered a paved courtyard enclosed on four sides by a large barracks. In a corner of the courtyard was a white mountain of newly carved sabots. At this time my conception of prisoner-of-war life was inaccurate, but this courtyard was the kind of place I had expected. Groups sat and lay near the stone walls. There were Moroccans and Senegalese. The groups seemed purposeless but not without hope; they had a kind of immobile wariness.

The barracks, several stories high, contained long rooms fitted with wooden racks to store military equipment. Each rack had four platforms, built of thin wooden slats. There was such a rush to secure a place to sleep on the racks that they were overloaded. In the night the weight on top caused a rack to collapse and several men sleeping on the lower platforms were crushed to death.

During the following evening, for the first time, the German army took our names and army numbers in the courtyard of a technical school at Lokeren. Even so, people at home were not informed until at least two months later. We spent the night in the school and I, entering when most of the space had been taken, slept in the attic among plaster casts of Greek sculpture. In the attic there was also the advantage of straw. I found a notebook, a rare treasure, and made notes and drawings until it was confiscated in Germany. A measured drawing of a Doric column was added to my possessions.

Even the most optimistic of my group had disregarded the persistent rumour that we would board a train, but at Moerbeke (we had nearly crossed Belgium) we boarded open coal railway cars and were transported into Holland. It was a profitable two hour journey as our very slow progress allowed the Dutch people to hand up food and drink of the most varied and satisfying kinds. I can remember still a rice pudding that was poured into my tin. Those standing at the sides had the best chance and some few in that advantageous position handed something, now and then, to those jammed in the middle of the cars. But those away from the sides fared badly — and let us know it. This day and the day we marched to Béthune were the only days we had enough to eat. After the train journey we received a better meal than usual from the Germans — a cup of peas and a square inch of meat. No doubt those areas where the civilians were most generous were the areas with most food, and the Germans were better able to feed us.

Having lasted nearly three weeks the march itself was finished. The journey took a new form.

III

We had reached Walsorden. Marching up an avenue of tall trees we saw quite suddenly and unexpectedly a very wide expanse of water like the sea. It was the Scheldt and we boarded long coal barges moored against a quay. About fifteen hundred men went on each barge. The engine driven barges were some hundred feet long with a space to walk round the sides. Each crew had a cabin at the stern. The decks sloped upwards to a ridge, and at intervals hatches with steep ladders gave access to holds. I sat on the slope and stayed there day and night, except when I visited the latrine: one or two seats open to the sky on the top deck. When it rained the holds were so crowded that a man took up a crouching position on each rung of the ladder. Men were jammed in the holds so that no one could move. It was better, almost, to sit on top in the rain.

Before the barges crossed the river, on the morning of July 2nd, a loaf of black bread was issued to each man — his ration for four days.

I embarked with a feeling of relief and contemplated a stage of the journey without marching. It was a luxury to sit down and rest. But, after a day of sitting and lying in one place in wet clothes after rain and an interminable night of intense cold, I got very tired of it. The scenery on both sides was uninteresting — two grass banks for most of the journey, for we were not high enough to see the country beyond the banks. Some seals on a sandbank, and the town of Dordrecht are all I remember. There were, on the other hand, interesting sky effects. One evening the sun was setting behind the slowly-moving barge. The clouds resembled an enormous fire smouldering at a great distance. The only sound, while the rear cabin swung slowly across the sunset as the barge turned with the canal, was a continuous soft scraping, the never-ending movement of the French prisoners about the deck like a restless army of ants.

The holds had a thin layer of coal dust and lice were in the dust. Men who caught lice in these holds could not rid themselves of them for more than a month.

I avoided the holds and sat on the sloping deck reading the New Testament. In this way I escaped the lice.

The last part of the voyage was up the Rhine. We passed under several steel bridges that had been blown; neatly severed at their centres. The abutments had not been destroyed as they should have been, and the enemy could easily repair them. Then we entered Germany.

IV

We reached the German town of Emmerich on the evening of July 4th. The night was spent on the barge and we went ashore in row boats in the morning. Emmerich had all its flags flying. Officials in uniforms with gold and silver braid were everywhere and hundreds of people wore swastika armbands. The town was at the height of its glory. Later, towards the end of the war, Emmerich was reduced to ruins.

We waited in a football field near the railway until mid-afternoon. Then we boarded empty railway cattle cars. Guards shouting "Los, Los" hurried us with rifle butts.

Forty to forty-five men crowded into each cattle car which would be too full for a long journey with twenty men. At the ends about five feet from the floor a car had two small openings about six by eighteen inches. These openings were the only means by which fresh air could enter, or waste matter and water be ejected during the sixteen hour journey. After the heavy, sliding doors had clanged shut, they were not opened until we reached our destination. A little bread had been issued at Emmerich — but as usual, not nearly enough. We were weak. Those with dysentry, and they were numerous, suffered most. With no room to lie down or to change position often, in a dim light, with violent shaking or jolting, the sixteen hours passed slowly. As night drew on there were attempts to find an arrangement by which most of us could lie down while the rest sat with their legs drawn up. We tried rows closely packed across the floor. We tried rows parallel to the length of the car without success, and as no agreement could be reached, we went on as before. We lurched, got cramp, dozed off in excruciatingly uncomfortable positions throughout the night and were extremely relieved to get out at Ziegenhain Nord, near Treysa, a town we could see in the distance.

The station was in the country: there were few houses. Before we reached Ziegenhain camp we marched several miles along winding country roads. I remember a man and a woman in the traditional peasant dress. The woman wore an unbecoming small black hat like a miniature top hat. As we approached the camp, a number of negroes, French Equatorial troops, were levelling a field in a dilatory way. I thought if I were not forced to work harder than that the future might not be too bad: I was to be disappointed. What eventually happened to *les noirs* I have never heard. I saw none during my period of detention, or while in Germany after release. I am afraid few survived to become free men. I liked les noirs because they were always smiling.

Ziegenhain was a large Dulag or transit camp in several widely separated parts. The first, which we entered, the administration section, had a number of long, brick, one-storey buildings, some of them unfinished. Drawn up in a field we awaited a bath and our turn to have our clothing de-loused.

We were instructed to leave metal and leather articles such as mess tins, watches or belts in the field because they are affected by steam de-lousing. Everyone did not obey this order, but I dug a small hole in the turf in which I hid my watch, and on top placed the one or two books, papers and some French cigarettes I had bought on the march. A few at a time, we went into one of the buildings and undressed. All clothing was taken by French prisoners on the staff and placed in the steam de-lousing machines. We had a shower bath — the first bath for many weeks. They hurried us out to Frenchmen with hair clippers who not only clipped our heads so closely they looked shaved, but clipped all the hair from our bodies. Their surliness and roughness caused protests; they were called pro-German bastards and worse, but they had the advantage on us, and their job could not be considered pleasant. After rubbing in a burning oily lotion we passed into a large room full of wooden forms to dry and await our clothes.

Rows of naked, hairless men sitting on forms (some were gaunt and all had lost considerable weight) looked like a Martian parliament in session.

Dressed in our steaming, crumpled clothing we returned to the field to collect our belongings. Nearly everyone lost something; many lost their watches. Mine was still hidden under the turf, but my cigarettes had disappeared. The thieves were German guards.

Having completed this initiation we marched to another part of the camp filled with rows of large tents. When assigned to a tent we

36

tried to get enough space to lie down for it was crowded, and waited for a call to queue up for something to eat.

The rations were better than any we had received. A bowl of potato soup was luxurious fare. There were ways of getting bread from the cookhouse staffed by French and Belgian prisoners. The Belgians offered bread for watches and fountain pens. After spreading the rumour that fountain pens would be confiscated by the Germans, the Belgians obtained a fountain pen for a slice of bread. Watches changed hands at all prices from a slice of bread to a loaf. The Belgians were the only Belgian prisoners of war I saw or heard of during the war, except two or three I met in 1945.

There was a lack of water. A pipe with a tap stuck up out of the ground in the middle of the compound, but a queue a hundred yards long was always in waiting. Sometimes the water was turned off and it amused me to watch les noirs, who were always inordinately thirsty, sucking the tap to draw any drops still in the pipe. Les noirs were Senegalese perhaps, with three or four vertical incisions on each cheek. More picturesque were the Moroccans wearing dark red tarbooshes. I was so taken with these hats that I offered to buy one. The Moroccan refused. "C'est mon bébé," he explained.

The Moroccan soldiers made a market every evening in the road between the large tents. The scene was like a bazaar. Some had clothing over their arms for sale. Money not being highly valued, the price was a watch, fountain pen or some article of value. Here and there a group watched a gambling game, played with dice. "Et doublez, et doublez," howled a Moroccan, crosslegged on the ground. "Toujours et toujours, le numéro trois à gagner!"

The loafing, wandering crowd bartered and gambled. Rumours flared up. In five or six languages the shouting and talking continued until we were ordered into our tents for the night.

The Belgians thought they would be sent home in a week or two. One of them, a sergeant-major, acted as interpreter for the camp. From him I learned something of the German prisoner-of-war system. He said we would be sent out to small working camps called Kommandos from a main camp or Stammlager. The picture he gave us was brighter than the truth but not altogether false.

37

In reality, the country was divided into areas called Stalags usually designated by a numeral and letter, such as IXC. Every Stalag had a main camp from which it was administered and which served as a clearing house for those changing Kommandos, going to a Kommando from a hospital, and for men caught attempting to escape. Under the main camp, but often one or two hundred kilometres from it, were the Kommandos or working camps of about a hundred men, situated near a factory, mine or quarry where the men worked in the daytime and returned to the camp at night. A German N.C.O. from Unteroffizier to Feldwebel commanded each Kommando with the help of half a dozen or more guards. Often they had a bloodhound or Alsatian police dog. In a Stalag there were several Control Officers, also N.C.O.'s, each responsible for all the Kommandos in his district. However, there were Stalags containing British prisoners run on different lines. In these several thousand men lived in one large camp and were sent out daily in working parties, but I have no first hand knowledge of them.

British N.C.O.'s of the rank of corporal and above went to a large non-working camp. All airmen had non-working camps of their own. Officers were detained in Offlags and did not work. Army N.C.O.'s captured in 1940, however, were forced to work during the first few months of imprisonment, and all privates and lance-corporals were forced to work. There was no way of avoiding work except by going to a hospital.

My own Stalag, IXC, was international. Poles, French, Serbs and Russians (after they entered the war in 1941) had working camps of their own. All Russians under the rank of Colonel worked. Stalag IXC had two main camps. One, an administration centre at Bad Sulza in Thüringia, had only a few British prisoners after 1941 — the Chief British "Man of Confidence" and his helpers. (Man of Confidence is a literal translation of the German word Vertrauensmann.) Red Cross parcels and letters arrived at the Administration Centre to be allotted to the various working camps, between 30 and 40 in number. The other main camp at Molsdorf was later moved to an old brewery on the outskirts of Mühlhausen and served as the clearing house of the Stalag. IXC controlled 2800 to 3000 prisoners of war.

39

On the morning of July 8th we marched back to the cattle cars and after a journey much like that to Ziegenhain arrived at Bad Sulza in the evening. Bad Sulza is a small town on the main railway line near Weimar. It is a resort surrounded by high hills, a ruined castle standing on one of them. The long, one-storey brick Stalag administration buildings were being built by Polish prisoners. There were several hundred Poles in khaki uniforms with small red triangles stencilled on their backs. Their fine physique and bearing were impressive, but we were not allowed to mix with them: they were kept apart by barbed wire. They occasionally threw tobacco over the wire to us — a very friendly gesture.

That night we slept on wood shavings spread in large tents. The shavings stank of fish and lice appeared again. Either the de-lousing had not been thorough or there were lice in the shavings.

In the morning every man was photographed holding a number in front of him. They took our fingerprints, and we were interrogated in an administration building by polite English speaking German soldiers. Any money we handed in was recorded and receipts were given. We were searched and I lost my few books; even cigarette papers were confiscated. Every man was issued with an oblong zinc plate with P.O.W. number impressed in it to be hung round his neck on a piece of string. Men who hid articles under the earth inside the tent lost them as we were not allowed to return.

Those who spoke French were told to form up apart. My friends and I thought this might mean easier work so we joined this group. A young Feldwebel questioned everyone in turn.

"Where did you learn French?" I was asked. "A l'école?"

"Oui, à l'école," I replied, glad I was not put to a test.

A party was called out by number and marched about a mile to a one-storey building, the Hotel Eichenbaum, once a dance hall. It had a small garden, a patch of grass and one or two trees, in front. This place was preferable to the tents though it was grossly overcrowded and there were lice in the wood shavings covering the floor. The lavatory stank and its floor was so rotten that men sometimes fell through it into a foot or two of reeking filth. The Hotel Eichenbaum later became known as Hell's Kitchen. In spite of its drawbacks I preferred it to anywhere I had stayed. One could sit out on the grass and sometimes, under cover of a wash house, crawl into the neighbouring vegetable garden to steal onions and lettuces.

Some of us still had cigarette papers not found at the search and we made cigarettes of dried leaves or, if we could procure a few shreds of tobacco, a very thin cigarette was passed round. During the evenings German airmen came into the enclosure and tried to talk to us in spite of the language difficulty. Their visits were welcome because they usually handed out twenty or thirty cigarettes. In the evenings a calliope organ played in a carnival in the town. Time did not hang heavily on my hands at Hell's Kitchen except at night. The nights were always interminable.

The wash house was a great advantage. There was an opportunity not only to bathe, but to wash trunks and vests and to dry them on the grass.

Every morning, early, we marched down to the tents to receive a bowl of burnt grain coffee-water. At noon we went down for a bowl of potato or cabbage soup and again in the evening for a bread and margarine ration. Sometimes instead of margarine, there was cheese and, once or twice, ersatz honey. These visits did not satisfy our hunger — the quantities were small. We got into a habit of cutting our bread into small strips, or into minute cubes like dice, to make it last longer. Food was still the mainstay of conversation and there were long discussions about meals — a habit that persisted for several months.

On July 10th we received our first official cards to post home and felt better knowing that our relatives and friends would soon receive certain knowledge of us. The cards were printed in English and we were allowed to write "yes" or "no" against "wounded," "unwounded" and so on.

Complaints about lice lead to the eighty-six men at Hell's Kitchen being taken to Weimar where there was a steam de-lousing plant at a military hospital. We travelled in railway cattle cars. Weimar was bedecked with flags. Hitler's long, low, private railway carriage mounted with anti-aircraft guns stood in the station. He was there for an anniversary or speech but we did not see him.

At the hospital a young doctor with an earnest, humourless face tried to give us some Nazi propaganda while we waited to be de-

42

loused. There is no doubt he believed what he said. In the following years we heard much propaganda but it fell off towards the end. The Germans gave up the British prisoner of war as a hopeless case.

We had been at Hell's Kitchen several days when certain numbers were called and groups were sent to factories, quarries and salt mines though we who were left behind had no idea where they went. The French went to farms and the British to a sugar refinery, factories, stone quarries and salt mines. Later, the Serbs worked on farms and the Russians anywhere — often on the railways. There were some exceptions to these rules.

At last, on July 25th, my turn came. My number, 1697, by which I was to be known to the enemy for five years, was called, and in a group of one hundred I left Bad Sulza in a cattle car.

A WILDERNESS OF DAYS

I

The journey by cattle car was as intolerable as the journey to Bad Sulza, only by now we were used to this slow, jolting way of travelling. The train went west, passing through the city of Erfurt. We reached our destination about eleven o'clock the same night.

Unterbreizbach has some fifteen hundred people. The station is separated from the main part of the town, old half-timbered and plastered buildings on cobbled streets, by the Ulster River and its twentieth-century concrete bridge. It was too dark to see anything not silhouetted against the sky, as we marched the mile to the camp, three abreast. We remained on the station side of the river; saw black outlines of pit-head wheels and factory chimneys. A few minutes later appeared flat, triangular shapes like huge slag heaps. The word went round that it was a coal mine.

The camp was two long, one-storey wooden barracks separated by a wide cinder path. I was among the first twenty men to enter the first section of the barracks. The others were put in four rooms farther along. It was a working camp: Arbeits Kommando 137.

First impressions were good. The twenty-foot square room had an electric light (we had been without light for months) and ten, two-tier wooden beds. A central stove separated two large tables with long benches, and each bed had an upright wooden cupboard against the wall beside it. I had an argument with a man I did not know; we claimed the same bed. It was a mistake; the upper bed was unclaimed and thus began a long, pleasant association, for we shared a cupboard and food until the end of the war, although for the greater part in room five. For this first night we were in room one at the west end of the camp.

Outside, on the wide, cinder path, the works manager of the mine and Klotzbach, the civilian caterer — a man about thirty-five with a plump face and rosy complexion (we disliked both on sight), stood talking to three prisoners who understood German. We heard that it was a salt mine.

One of those who spoke German became our interpreter for all official purposes when, next day, the man of highest military rank became the Man of Confidence. He was our head-man, a Bandmaster, the highest non-commissioned rank in the British Army. An educated man, with the help of the interpreter, he often successfully resisted the Kommandant, Control Officer and the civilian officials of the Company, the Sachsen-Weimar branch of the powerful Kali Syndicate, and not least, the cunning Klotzbach who, during five years, kept up a continual battle with the camp.

Two blankets, a white china soup bowl and a spoon were issued to every man. The two tier beds had wood bed slats to support a straw mattress and a straw filled pillow case. I believe only once during the five years was there a fatigue to empty the mattresses and fill them with fresh straw. By that time the straw was a mass of short pieces without resilience. There were never any bugs at 137. The buildings were fairly new when we first occupied them.

We, as a camp, put pressure on the enemy for observance of the Geneva Convention as soon as we became aware of its articles (some months after our arrival) and for better living and working conditions. In later years, three Kommandants tried to help us, but when one worked too hard on our behalf the Kali Syndicate used its influence to remove him.

In the five years we had fifteen or sixteen Kommandants — most stayed about three months, some nearly a year. The five or six guards adopted the attitude of the Kommandant towards us so that a good Kommandant meant good guards. The Man of Confidence often negotiated directly when the language was sufficiently mastered, but during the first year the interpreter was always present.

At Appells, or roll-calls, parleys often took place. The Kommandant complained and made demands countered as best they could by the Bandmaster and Len Keys, our interpreter. We never referred to the Bandmaster by name — always as the "Bandmaster". The

Kommandant's words were interpreted to the long line of prisoners drawn up in the Dining Hall. Some Commandants took pleasure in sallies of wit at our expense, or in reviewing us, and in various ways showing off. They got tired of it after a few weeks and held Appells less often. But a new Kommandant usually began it all again. The tall, dignified Bandmaster managed to make these Kommandants seem ridiculous. Always erect and neatly dressed he appeared very different from our Jewish interpreter, short, vivacious, never still, dressed often in underwear shorts with his shirt half out. They were a formidable team, the Bandmaster extremely firm, courteous, confident; the interpreter quick-witted and aggressive. It was thought that a certain protest about working conditions would be stronger if it were put in a letter written by the Bandmaster to the Kommandant and presented at an Appell. The letter was in German and opened with greetings from the camp. The interpreter solemnly read out an English version to us. The letter succeeded.

In the morning after our arrival, the slag heaps became flat conical wooded hills. Three-quarters of a mile south of us, across the small Ulster River, a large wheel revolved slowly above red brick and galvanized iron buildings. A railway bridge crossed the river to the west, near the camp gates, used by Company engines to haul coal, bricks and machinery to the mine, and carloads of salt to Unterbreizbach station. The town could not be seen from the camp.

Some men made playing cards of cardboard scraps during our first day at the camp. Not for a day or two did prisoner-of-war numbers arrive from the mine office assigning us to jobs and dividing us into one morning and one afternoon shift. I was in the morning shift. The afternoon shift went first at about 1:30 p.m. and returned at 11:30.

The following morning at 3:15 a.m. my turn came. Padlocks and bars were noisily removed by a guard. In the Dining Hall, at a hatch in the kitchen wall, we received two slices of heavy gray bread, bright red ersatz jam tasting of chemicals and a bowl of burnt grain coffee. The shift was drawn up in threes on the cinder path. It was dark; the guards had flashlights. Two guards with fixed bayonets marched us across the concrete bridge to the village and up a long gradual hill to the mine gate-house. The leading guard's flashlight made quivering circles of light on the road. Inside the gate-house we inserted cards with our P.O.W. numbers in the time-clock. This was the first time in my life I had punched a card.

The mine yards are large, and after marching a quarter of a mile we entered a room reserved for surface workers to change their clothes and eat *Frühstück*. Such rooms were always called Frühstück rooms. Here workers eat a slice or two of bread during the half-hour break in an eight-hour shift. Frühstück means breakfast, but the break was always Frühstück whatever the time of day or night.

Several foremen arrived, and we were split up and assigned to various jobs. Six men, including myself, were taken away by a civilian foreman. We began to stack bricks in a large concrete building, partly gutted by fire.

During our few weeks in Germany we had learned some words, notably "nicht verstehen", a convenient way passively to resist orders. But we couldn't depend on "don't understand" for many days.

I advised my companions to move and work as slowly as possible. Such advice was hardly necessary after weeks of semi-starvation. The time passed more slowly that day, and during the days that followed until I became used to manual work, than ever before or since. The foreman stood watching us for the whole shift during the first weeks. But work at the mine was always a minute-counting existence for me. Nearly four years later I worked with a gang under a German foreman laying nine-inch water pipe outside the village where the time didn't drag so much, and there was the occasional day moving some piece of machinery or coal to another village. After the first year I could do hard physical work without tiring, but for the first few months I reached the camp exhausted after an eight-hour shift and lay on my bed.

A factory whistle blew at 1:30 p.m. — the end of the morning shift. A shift lasted eight hours — eight and a half hours with Frühstück. For a year in the middle of the war we worked a ten-hour shift.

Back at the camp on that first day we lined up with our bowls at the hatch in the *Speisesaal* (Dining Hall). Two women employed by Klotzbach filled our bowls with a dipper from the boiler. The soup

was mainly potato with some small pieces of fat or meat. Some handfuls of caraway seeds had been thrown in.

For eight or nine months we sat at tables in the Speisesaal for our soup. When Red Cross parcels came we began to take our soup to our rooms. The Germans objected at first, but permission was obtained by the Man of Confidence, and thereafter all meals were eaten in the rooms. The Speisesaal became a place of recreation only, and a place to hold Appells in very cold or wet weather.

After the first month, the Kommandant found jobs for us during our spare time. One of these was to make flower beds along the buildings on each side of the cinder path. The edges were made with bricks on edge. No one felt like doing this before or after a shift at the mine. The Bandmaster got the Kommandant to agree to a rota so that only half a dozen men worked at it each day. The flower beds were finished after a fashion and abandoned. Strangely, no one in a camp of very varied interests wanted to grow flowers, yet there was at least one professional gardener among us. Cleaning out the three-foot diameter soup boiler was another fatigue in our first year. Later the two kitchen women had to do it.

Twice, soon after arrival at the camp, all went with the guards to a military hospital for de-lousing. We went by train to Meiningen and Eisenach. Shifts of ten entered the hospital, stripped and deposited all clothing in the steam room, while the rest waited in the hospital grounds. During one of these trips the camp was cleaned by French prisoners. They stole many of our personal belongings, although we had little enough in those early days. The Bandmaster and interpreter protested so strongly that this kind of visitation never occurred again.

For three and a half years I worked with the transport gang, known as Göbel's gang. Göbel was the civilian *Meister* or foreman. The six British prisoners assigned to him called him Göbel, pronounced Gable in the Thüringian dialect. He used our Christian names pronounced as if German. I haven't much fault to find with him, considering that the works manager (*Betriebsführer*) and directors kept constant pressure on all Meisters to increase production. Our work was heavy. The transport gang unloaded everything that came by rail, and a great part of what was taken away, except

the salt. Some coal was unloaded by the *Kesselhaus* (Boiler House) gang, but we unloaded hundreds of cars of steam coal, coke and briquettes. New brick buildings were built, and a chimney a hundred metres high. Unloading and stacking bricks was a transport job. A line of four or five men threw bricks one to another from the railway car to the stack. At first bricks rubbed skin off my fingers. The Germans showed us a rhythmic way of throwing and catching bricks, and the job became easy. In later years emptying a car of coal was exhilarating, when the weather was fine. These jobs had to be done in all weathers. After three years we were relieved of coal to a great extent. A large grab was installed and operated by the boiler house gang.

The early days were the worst. Any job became comparatively easy after long practice. Shovelling refuse into a truck was a transport job, and the longhandled German shovels used against the left thigh need a certain apprenticeship. Shovelling salt had the same technique.

The transport gang never knew where it would be working the next day — an advantage we thought. Work was less boring that way. Sometimes we worked outside the grounds of the mine. There were jobs in every building and part of the surface and occasionally down in the mine. In the mine, half a mile below the surface, we moved drums of wire-rope. We loaded the drums on the elevator cage controlled by the great wheels above the shaft. One elevator cage went down as the other came up. Nearly every day a man accompanied empty oxygen and acetylene containers on a fifteen kilometre truck drive to Merkers, said to be the largest salt mine in the world. About thirty steel containers were loaded empty on the truck, unloaded at Merkers, and full containers loaded and unloaded. There is a way to handle these containers that has to be learned. They are unwieldy and can crush a man's hand. The job was liked for the ride and consequent inactivity even in the company of the morose and lazy German driver. This Kaiseroda salt mine at Merkers was one of the mines used to hide treasure and paintings. In April 1945 American soldiers found five hundred and fifty canvas bags of gold Reichmarks, four hundred bags of gold brick and a number of boxes full of gold dental fillings and wedding rings from the concentration camps of Auschwitz and Buchenwald.

Felix, a Polish civilian attached to the gang, often helped to load and unload the gas containers. Felix had married a German woman and settled at Unterbreizbach before the war. He was short and wore a gray-green, first war army jacket that nearly reached his knees. He felt the inferiority of his origin in German eyes and was a toady and informer. I remember him lurking behind a concrete pillar in the burnt-out building, stamping his feet to keep warm on the tile floor, wet with salty water and slime, torn between laziness and the wish to distinguish himself in the eyes of Göbel. Felix was always with us, despised by all.

One of our worst and most frequented work places was the *Schrottplatz*. This scrap-iron yard was a dump of old valves, pumps, steel plate, iron wheels, broken cast-iron and machinery to be loaded into railway coal cars. Filling *Schrottwagen* was a transport job, as was taking the scrap to the dump. We filled two or three coal cars a week, sometimes for months on end, in all seasons. A car was full if it weighed twenty-two tons when pushed by our shoulders onto the weighing machine, the platform of which was a section of track long enough to accommodate a railway car. In winter the scrap was covered with snow. Then, and in the drizzling rain, the metal was greasy and slippery. There was no crane at the Schrottplatz. Everything was man-handled aboard, much of it heavy, moved on wooden rollers or pieces of pipe by crow-bars.

But the heap of old, frayed, salt-rotted wire-rope from the mine caused even more discomfort. It was loaded on flat cars. First it was pulled on the heap with iron hooks out of wooden tubs on wheels from the mine shaft. A yard engine pulled it on a flat car by a system of pulleys and wire-rope. The rope often broke when the mass of wire was only half on.

Next to the Schrottplatz was a large wooden storehouse full of machinery parts and drums of cable. A loading platform was on the railway side. Herr Sontag, in charge of stores, in a long white cotton coat, inspected or made inventories. German workmen or prisoners spent an unnecessarily long time in the warehouse. Sontag or anyone could be heard pushing back a sliding door to enter, and the group pretended to work.

No Egyptian slave used rollers to move heavy objects more than the transport gang or, after several years of practice, knew better how to use them. Sometimes they were logs, sometimes metal pipes. Three other tools were in constant use: the chain pulley, the jack and the crowbar. The jack is a *Winde* in German. The Winden, of different sizes, were wound up and down by a rotary handle, and the three-ton Winde was very heavy on the shoulder when carried half a mile, or up several flights of steps. I carried it up five flights a number of times. The crowbar is called an *Eisen*, an iron; straight without a crook at the end. Chain pulleys were of various sizes, a system of gears operated by an endless chain. When pulling heavy boilers or transformers, weighing sometimes fifteen tons or more, several men pulled the chain and the object inched its way into place. During our first winter, without gloves, but with the hand-rag German workmen carry called a *Lappen*, we suffered some hardship with these chains. In the second winter the temperature was 40 degrees below zero Fahrenheit one day when we pulled the chain, a brazier at the chain pulley and another beside us. I burnt several pairs of trousers by standing too close to the braziers, old gasoline drums, pierced and full of red hot coke. It was never so cold again, but there were many days when we worked in deadly cold weather using old socks as gloves. I received heavy leather working gloves from Canada in our third year. They lasted three weeks. Chains, bricks, scrap-iron and the rotting action of the salt destroyed them.

It took several weeks to remove several large steel cylindrical tanks lying on steel girders high up in the burnt-out building. They were lifted up and lowered by using chains and wire-rope attached to a winch on the ground. One had to use crowbars and Winden on a girder forty feet above the tile floor. Luckily no-one fell. I much preferred working at the winch which two men wound by hand.

One winter the gang cleared the road to Merkers in places where the snow had drifted. Without a daily supply of oxygen and acetylene containers the engineers couldn't attend to the constant need for machinery repairs caused by the destructive action of wet salt on metal.

From flat cars large steel pipes about a foot in diameter and twenty-feet long were unloaded. Pipes were rolled down to two logs propped against the flat car. Boards were laid on pipes already unloaded, and a pipe was rolled into place on these by two or three men. On fine days the job was not bad, especially when Göbel went away for a time. His broad figure in a cream-coloured work suit could be seen half a mile away returning along the tracks of the railway yard. In 1943 there was a shortage of rolling stock and cars had to be unloaded and taken away six hours after arrival. This caused overtime and Sunday work. If possible, Göbel found work under cover when it rained.

Baling waste paper from the offices was an odd job on Göbel's gang. Paper was dumped into a box every day and one of us helped old Winter, a short, round-shouldered workman with a deeply lined face, to press the paper and wire it into tight bales about three feet cube. It was done on an exposed concrete yard enclosed by a wire fence, a windy, cold place in full view of the offices. These bales had to be lifted into railway cars with a pulley. Winter, one of the best German civilians at the mine, often had a man assigned to him to visit the station across the railway bridge about a mile from the mine. We loaded a few crates or machinery parts on a flat car, sat in the station shed smoking or having a nap, always permitted by Winter when he thought it was safe, while he gossipped in the station. In good weather this was the best of jobs. In 1940 Winter shared his cigarettes with his helper and wasted as much time as possible. But his work had to be done. Who could ask for more?

Sometimes Winter worked in the *Eisenlager*, or iron storehouse, next to the waste-paper yard. We spent long hours sorting and stacking steel strips up to twenty-one feet long (four, five, six, seven metre lengths) and varying in weight. The strips were unloaded at the track running behind the storehouse and brought inside. Every one was upended against the brick wall of the Lager. Some strips and angles were so unwieldy that two, or even three men settled the menacing whipping ends high up against the wall. Later this iron was transferred to wooden racks in the centre of the storehouse. The ends were inserted in openings and the steel was pushed home against the friction set up by other pieces.

To a depth of two or three inches the dirt floor was covered with fine dust, as fine as cement dust. It rose and spurted in plumes round our feet.

Difficult and dangerous to handle were the *Bleche*, steel plates that were brought in from the railway and upended in racks. We wrestled with steel plates, about six feet by four feet most of them, for hours at a time. Fingers could be mashed by Bleche.

Sometimes a *Waggon* of steel rods up to five inches in diameter was unloaded and the rods placed. Four to six men moved large rods with tongs. A tong required two men who should be the same height and strength, but at the best are awkward to use. Much of this stock was loot from France.

Prisoners were outdone in passive resistance by two gypsies, *Zigeuner*, working for Göbel for several months. They annoyed us by avoiding their turn to pull the heavy Schrottwagen to and from the Schrottplatz. It was impossible to make them do their share, but their antics were amusing. I liked their dark, sharp features and carefree natures. They drove Johann, a German foreman under Göbel, wild with rage. Johann was a tremendous worker, the most energetic I have ever seen, consumed with zeal, either with ambition to become a Meister or to avoid military service. He was an asset to us because he did so much of the work himself. He disliked us and we disliked him. Arguments approaching violence were common. I once reported him to the Kommandant for knocking me down but nothing happened. The gypsies were sent away, probably to somewhere much worse, but their performance was surpassed by an American captured at Dieppe (Canadian Army) called "Alabama". He simulated insanity while with Göbel's gang, an elaborately overacted part which was successful after several weeks. Alabama was sent to a hospital.

When Johann left for military service, Niebel, an older man, short and very strong, became foreman under Göbel. It was said he had been a communist. He was missing for a week and we heard the Gestapo had taken him for questioning. But, unlike some Germans, he told us nothing, speaking only of the work at hand. Perhaps he found it too risky to talk much to prisoners of war, or seem to be sympathetic to them.

Göbel, with his shiny peaked workman's cap and shaved bullet head, reminded me of a Dutch barge owner. He roared with anger or grinned happily as occasion demanded. By nature genial in a rough way, he liked to bellow at some other Meister or foreman in what seemed to be a violent quarrel — but after several exchanges he turned to us and beamed from ear to ear. The German workmen enjoyed shouting at each other, although this game was not at first understood by us. Sometimes these dramatic rages became ridiculous as when a Meister in charge of welders and other technicians habitually threw his hat on the ground and stamped on it. Shouting, freely indulged among themselves, caused trouble sometimes when directed at prisoners who took it seriously. Knocking a German workman or foreman down could lead to serious consequences. This happened several times but was not always reported. Some fuss was made when it was, but I don't remember an incident when action was taken. But, in one of these quarrels, a prisoner said that Hitler was a swine. He went to trial at Kassel having, as we heard, a lawyer to defend him. He was sentenced to work at a German barracks for two years. We heard later that he had an easier time there than at 137.

The Löserhaus had seven floors where salt was processed in various large tanks and machines. Göbel's gang brought in new machinery and removed worn out parts at a wide door at each floor served by an electrically driven hook that ran up and down. Driving the crane on the seventh floor was a fairly pleasant job.

Sometimes in the fourth year, when I had a light worker's card, I counted steel tubs of unprocessed salt. They passed in an endless procession. I sat on a high stool at a desk. The tubs were drawn on tracks by wire-ropes from the mine shaft to machinery which turned the tubs over to empty the rock salt into huge silos. Each tub number was entered in my ledger as it came past. Often it had to be checked with a wooden club placed on the track in front of a wheel because the tubs crowded too close to see their numbers. About seven hundred tubs a day weighing two tons when full of salt came up from the mine. Counting the tubs was a Löserhaus job, but another gang pushed empty tubs in a large area with a floor of steel plates. Tubs could be turned and manoeuvred on this floor, greasy with wet salt, and pushed into the elevators for return to the mine.

In the autumn the transport gang filled sacks with coal and coke, loaded them on a truck and dumped them in cellars belonging to higher mine officials. It was easy to carry the sacks on the back, scrambling with them to the tops of the coal piles was exhausting. The gang collected garbage from these houses, and from the Polish prisoners quarters behind an old evil smelling dance hall in the town.

For several days we did a unique job. We transported packing cases of books from Karlsruhe from the railway to the mine elevators for safe storage in the mine. The books did not seem to be particularly valuable; several found their way to the camp — textbooks on engineering and mathematics.

In the mornings, a little after four in the summer, Göbel, or more often his head German workman, came down the concrete steps to the large Frühstück room where we changed into working clothes (after the first year, overalls were issued), or into an old uniform. We gave our work card to Göbel to be placed in a rack outside his "office". Nearby was the *Bude*, a closet with chains and ropes hanging on pipes, several jacks, steel pulleys and crowbars. It made me think of a medieval torture chamber. Every man had to take an Eisen or Winde. Often we took the Schrottwagen, a strong cart on iron wheels with solid rubber tires pulled by a long iron handle.

There were many jobs on the surface and in the mine that I never did. There were some fifteen hundred German workers, about a hundred British prisoners, a hundred to three hundred other workers, at different times Ukrainians and Bulgarians. How the office allocated jobs I don't know; the smallest men often had the heaviest jobs. Half the original one hundred British prisoners went down the mine in cages operated by huge wheels above the shaft. Below they dispersed to the tunnels, some of them more than a mile from the pit-head. They emerged at the end of a shift white with salt dust to have a shower in their Frühstück room: a different place from that of the surface workers. Miners all took carbide lamps; there was electric light only in the main thoroughfares or *Strecken*. The deepest part of the mine, more than half a mile, was hot and called Madiera by the Germans. The initial allocation held good throughout our detention. Occasionally a miner obtained a doctor's order to work above ground, but not without difficulty. Some preferred the mine, especially in the winter.

The Sachsen-Weimar mine was better than some others to work in. Men came to us from Craja where the rock salt ceilings of wide

60

tunnels were very high and dark. Pieces of rock salt of all sizes up to several tons dropped off the ceilings. Several men were hit — one had his back broken. Work went on through every shift with the possibility of rock salt dropping at any moment.

The best jobs were inside buildings on the surface, but there were few of these jobs. One was to test samples of salt in solution and note the readings at hourly intervals. Germans did this until, in the middle of the war, they were called up for military service. Light duties attending machines fell to prisoners in the Löserhaus about 1943. These jobs were incredibly boring. One could learn lines for plays and read cautiously. If caught reading by the Betriebsführer, or asleep, one would be put on a heavy job. For a time I had one of the light jobs. One of my duties was to grease a very heavy axle about three inches in diameter. Unfortunately for me the axle broke some time after I had the job. There was vague talk of sabotage and I was put back on Göbel's gang. I accosted the Betriebsführer several times and protested to the Kommandant, but I had to stay on the Transport Gang although no definite charge was made.

I never had a job loading salt in box cars. A dozen men formed a gang picking up bags the size of cement sacks. They slid down a metal shoot and men took them on their forearms and stacked them in the cars. This gang was called the *Verladung*. The empty paper sacks were unloaded by Göbel's gang, one of our lighter jobs.

The Verladung filled cars with loose salt also, after lining the cars with coarse building paper, so that the salt wouldn't seep away between the boards. Scenery for plays and revues was painted on this paper at the camp. The car was filled through a metal pipe, the nozzle put inside the door of the box car.

In the Verladung building processed fertilizer salt was stored in great piles from conveyor belts which could be heard in the camp at night. They made shrill, wailing sounds like lost souls. It was here "the sailor", one of our original hundred, was threatened with a bayonet and forced to do some job he had refused to do. It was in the early days, one of the first "incidents".

Those with unpleasant jobs, most of the prisoners, the Russian soldiers, Polish and Ukrainian slave labourers, went as often as possible to the lavatories. These were two some distance apart, with

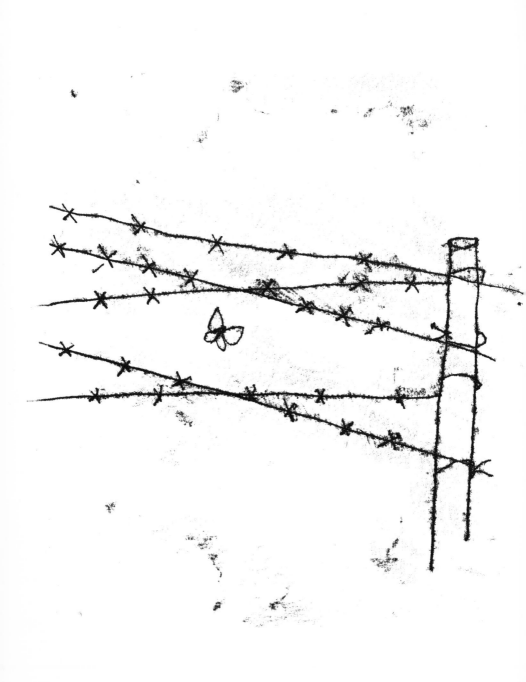

red tile floors always dirty and wet. One could smoke for a few minutes, keeping alert in case the Betriebsführer or a Meister looked in. Someone with news might be there. Rumours and news were spread in the lavatories, an important element in our working day, in spite of the wetness and the smell.

Göbel's gang was always on the morning shift, work starting before dawn in the winter. Dawn was beautiful. Sometimes the pink light called by the Germans *Morgenrot*, sometimes the bars of cool, pale gold that are not seen at any other time, appeared in the sky. At the mine I often looked at the rounded, fir-tree covered mountain called Oechsenberg where, on clear days, other British prisoners could be seen, although three miles away and hardly discernible against the sky, tipping wagons from a shelf in the mountain side. It was a stone quarry.

Several acres of iron vats full of wet salt were emptied and cleaned out at intervals. Shovelling hardened salt at the bottom of these flattish tanks was a fairly easy job. An escaping prisoner, hiding under the vats, was one day found by a search party of some thirty youths who worked at the mine for a month or two (*Hitlerjugend*, wearing brown uniforms with swastika armbands). They were lads of fifteen or sixteen armed with shovels instead of rifles. We expected much trouble from them as fanatical Nazis, but they surprised us. Many of them tried to dodge work. They marched to and from the mine singing the German marching songs, among them "Wir fahren gegen England."

Very often pumps in the Löserhaus broke down. These we carried on our wagon to the engineer's work shop, a large building fitted with cranes running on overhead girders and full of metal workers lathes. Nearly all the machinists were German.

II

Prisoners reported sick to avoid work. The mine management, through the Kommandant, tried to prevent malingering. They telephoned him about men absent from work, and put pressure on the local German civilian doctor who attended the camp. Dr. Schrader was not badly disposed towards us. Germans at the mine told us he had been the camp doctor during the first world war. A row of stone crosses stood in the cemetery at Unterbreizbach over British graves. Whatever Dr. Schrader's feelings were about us he never showed them, and he was more lenient than we had a right to expect. The directors of Sachsen-Weimar were anything but lenient, and the mine controlled the village.

Every morning a party, from two to fifteen men, marched under guard the mile to the doctor's house. Interviewed one by one, they were given one, two or more days in the camp. The doctor sometimes ordered a willing patient to bed until he made his weekly visit. Occasionally a man was sent straight back to work under guard.

In later years this did not often happen because a former Royal Army Medical Corps orderly was allowed to remain in the camp in charge of the sick. He and the Man of Confidence tried to prevent healthy men going sick too frequently; others might then have an occasional rest, and the sick could stay in the camp without continual trouble from the factory and the Kommandant.

Always anxious to hear the doctor's verdict when several pleasant days in camp were at stake, I yet found it interesting to look at German illustrated magazines in his waiting room. German civilians, usually women, took their turn with us. The doctor was an obstetrician. His bald head, clipped moustache and patient expression betrayed neither his age nor his feelings. He spoke no English.

The orderly was called *Sanitätor* by the Germans. He accompanied us to the doctor and used his German medical vocabulary on our behalf. His German, acquired at the factory and camp, was fluent but inaccurate. Dr. Schrader usually took his word.

For a year, the original one hundred men suffered from boils. Several suffered greatly, boil after boil came to a head, some as large as an egg. Unless very bad, boils did not allow a man to get on the sick list and the dirt and salt of the mine aggravated the condition.

Not many months passed after our arrival before a man got ill enough to be sent to hospital. He had to be very ill to go, but the precedent once set, it was never again too difficult for a sick man to reach hospital. Usually someone was waiting to go, or had just returned with news or other interesting information.

The hospitals that served our camp, called Reserve Lazarets, were at Obermassfeld, Meiningen and Hildburghausen, all three staffed by British medical officers, themselves prisoners, under a *Stabsarzt* — a German military doctor. The Germans tried to send men back to work, sometimes before they were well. When large scale air attacks began it became necessary to make room for wounded airmen, Commonwealth and American. Often their condition was extremely serious. Meiningen took in more than two hundred airmen in one day at short notice. Many of these men had to be operated on, and the strain on six or eight doctors was almost unbearable.

These hospitals had been built for other purposes: Meiningen a casino, Hildburghausen a private asylum (part of it was still kept for civilian mental cases). I was examined twice at real hospitals at Eisenach but prisoners never stayed there.

In the spring of 1942 I had gastric trouble for many weeks. After being off work ten days I was told to go to hospital early next morning with all my possessions. After two years these amounted to a full kitbag and my haversack. I had collected books by this time, heavy to carry but too valuable to be left behind. When discharged from hospital I might be sent to another camp.

A German guard and the Sanitäter accompanied me to Hildburghausen. Train journeys were always interesting, in spite of long periods of waiting on station platforms when we changed trains. German civilians took litttle notice of us. They were, most of them, emotionally unaffected by our British uniforms. The British prisoner felt himself superior to the Germans. This "mystique" held our little band together and presented a united front to the enemy. It needed no propaganda, no agitation to maintain itself and presents an interesting psychological outlook. Whatever the reason, morale could not have been higher. Civilians sometimes passed a few remarks with us, and I noticed the slight feeling of having something in common, the bond of *der kleine Mann*. It was understood in these rather inarticulate conversations that we were all victims of an inscrutable authority — mere pawns. Civilians offered their seats to prisoners once when several of us entered a crowded carriage.

The trains that conveyed us to the hospitals were slow, local trains; the passengers villagers and country people. I liked their apple-red

faces, the women with black, shawl-covered heads, the sturdy, thick-fingered, honest countrymen, elderly and provincial.

Mainline trains were different. The people were preoccupied, less simple and kindly. On these trains prisoners were ignored, taken as a matter of course, in my experience. But an old and better Germany seemed to exist, resigned and inarticulate, in the villages and small market towns. For instance, when working outside the mine grounds, laying pipe beside a road, no countryman or woman passed on foot or on a bicycle without giving us a greeting.

During these journeys we met prisoners from other camps. Waiting on the same platform we exchanged information. Our guards received a few cigarettes from us (after March 1941, the Red Cross sent food parcels and cigarettes) and often allowed these conversations.

Hildburghausen was a five-hour journey. Marching on the cobbled street was heavy going with my overcoat and baggage. At that time an order required prisoners and their guards to keep off the sidewalks, and walk in the road. The hospital, known as the *Karolinenburg*, one of the buildings of the old asylum, was at the opposite side from the station of the hilly, steep-roofed town. We reached the woods and fields surrounding the Karolinenburg and entered its courtyard guarded by a helmeted soldier at a black, white and red striped sentry box.

I was shown into a washroom in the basement, and had a bath while my clothes and baggage were de-loused. An English orderly told me to stay there until fetched, leaving me a cup of cocoa. A barred window was not too high for me to see sunlit trees and blue sky. Here were the conical hills I had become accustomed to near Unterbreizbach. The quietness gave me a feeling of freedom, of rest. There was time to reflect.

On his return I showed the orderly that I had vomited the cocoa. This, as I hoped, was reported to the doctors.

I took a Wasserman for venereal disease and was weighed. Weight was important. When the Stabsarzt looked for men to send back to work the scales were his weapon. Malingering can be an art but it is impossible when weighed stripped to cheat the scales. Additional weight meant regained health to the Stabsarzt.

The supply of Red Cross food parcels and invalid comfort parcels to hospitals was regular and plentiful. Cigarettes were comparatively abundant. Letters arrived regularly at 137; at hospitals the mail was uncertain — one of the few drawbacks.

My doctor, a former Harley Street specialist, put me on a diet that did me good from the first. I shared a room with a Serb. We played chess with a set I had carved from pieces of wood picked up at the mine. There were several real sets in the recreation room. The Serb and I conversed in an international jargon of French, German and English and I missed him when he departed to an unknown destination.

There were two other Serbs, patients who had managed to take on permanent positions as pressers of uniforms, laundrymen and servants of the doctors. Chopanov, inveterate trader, black-marketeer and amusing rogue, sat for a pencil portrait, his army cap at a smart angle and his large black moustache ends pointing upwards.

In the evenings the RAMC sergeant-major called out the numbers for Bingo in professional style. To enter cost a cigarette. The prizes were cigarettes, Turkish with a small green star and crescent. Cigarettes had been scarce at Arbeits Kommando 137; parcels to individuals did not arrive for another year or more.

These were relatively happy days. I should have been glad to stay at the Karolinenburg until the end of the war.

The Stabsarzt believed in cold feet and hands in stomach cases. I was nervous of the result of a patient by patient inspection a week after my arrival. He hardly noticed me. His weekly visits were preceded by much cleaning up and floor-washing. Anyone on the danger list spent time in the washroom scrubbing nicotine stains off his fingers. Smoking was strictly forbidden in the wards, and at all times for heart and stomach cases. Tobacco stains condemned a man if the Stabsarzt was in a bad humour. Needless to say everyone smoked when he felt like it.

Great preparations were made for a General who did not arrive. Old patients remembered several such scares.

Down a corridor, outside the main door to the wards was a room with a sink and three electric hot plates. Walking patients cooked here and heated tins from their Red Cross parcels. All meals came from the huge central kitchen of the asylum near the Frauenhaus, another hospital building, the surgical section. These meals could be augmented by the parcels. There was rather too much than too little food at the Karolinenburg. Two or three walking patients fetched the containers of hot food in hand carts, and I graduated to this fatigue in the course of time.

A barred window in the room with the hot-plates looked out on the courtyard. Civilian mental cases lined up here every morning, and attendants took them to work in neighbouring fields. These poor people hated the Englanders and shook their fists at us as we watched from the window.

One morning, rather early, from this window I saw a column of men marching in the road outside the gates. They were Polish prisoners being taken under guard to witness the execution by hanging of twenty-one fellow prisoners. Two Poles had escaped and killed a German policeman. They, with nineteen others, were hanged as an example, every Pole in the vicinity being forced to attend. This execution depressed all of us at the hospital, or rather, forced us into a savage, frustrated state of mind that lasted two or three days.

I had been told of another affair concerning the Poles while working with old Winter. Winter owned an inn or *Gasthaus* in his village in which he was forced to house twenty Polish prisoners of war and be responsible for their rations. They worked on nearby farms. One morning he told me that his Poles had gone.

"Soldiers arrived", he said, "and the Poles having just finished their supper were lined up. A Feldwebel called for volunteers for the German army to step forward. No one moved. The first Pole in line was told to volunteer. He refused and was beaten up. The Feldwebel offered encouragement to volunteer by threatening to gouge the eyes out of any who refused. It was essential that they volunteer."

Before the Poles were taken from Winter's village, one of them named as her lover by a pregnant German woman, was bound to her with rope and forced to walk with her up the village street. She had her head shaved and went to prison. He was executed. I believed Winter's medieval stories.

We liked the Poles knowing which side they were on.

In hospitals, as in all camps, the "Combine" or "Syndicate" system prevailed. Usually a patient confined to bed was a member of a syndicate for sharing Red Cross parcels with at least one walking patient in it. He collected all their parcels once a week. Parcels were given out by a German guard in the basement and they were kept under beds or on the lower shelves of bedside tables.

At certain times, between two and three in the afternoon and by nine-thirty in the evening, all patients had to be in bed. A few bed patients were content never to get up, although only about twenty years old. So afraid of being sent to a salt mine or quarry were some young men that any improvement in their condition was cause for alarm; any worsening, if the effects were noticeable, cause for optimism, almost of rejoicing. Some of them were serious heart cases. I thought of *The Magic Mountain* by Thomas Mann in which patients in a sanatorium in the Alps dreaded a return to the "flatland" and the worries, exertion and responsibility that they would find there. To some extent we all shared this desire to remain. Before a visit of the German doctor to the wards everyone was anxious, especially if we expected a "purge". Afterwards those who escaped relaxed for a week or two.

One walking patient would have been sent out long before had he not established himself as the Stabsarzt's gardener. He worked several hours a week in this garden and his confidence in staying on until the end of the war was irritating. He didn't know the war would last another three years.

When I had enjoyed life at the Karolinenburg for five weeks, we heard that a purge was coming for all but the bed patients. With fourteen others a gain in weight put me on the work list. I played my last card, asking to be sent to Molsdorf, then the main camp of the Stalag from which men were assigned to working camps. I hoped to stay there a few weeks before I was sorted out. In this non-working camp men sometimes got lost and stayed month after month for no apparent reason. I managed with a little help from a British doctor to get my papers made out to Molsdorf. When presented to the Stabsarzt for his signature he was in a bad temper. He noticed the change and had the papers retyped for Arbeits Kommando 137.

I returned to the salt mine, my shoulders sore from my kitbag full of canned food and additional books. The other member of my hospital syndicate, suffering from severe arthritis, had also been sent out to a camp at a needle factory several hundred kilometres east.

At regular intervals I reported sick as a stomach case, not without reason, although the Karolinenburg had done me good. The bread issued as part of our rations, and sliced and apportioned by the "Room" on fatigue at the time, seemed to cause my indigestion. I found half burnt slivers of wood in it, and we believed the baker waged his own war with us by mixing sawdust with the dough. The grayish brown loaves were very heavy. A weekly fatigue, four or five men with a wooden farm wagon, fetched about a hundred loaves from the bakery in the village. A printed sign in the bakery stated that no Poles or Jews would be served. We usually got the bread from the cobblestoned courtyard behind the shop. Loaves were thrown from hand to hand and stacked in the cart. It was necessary to eat the bread, and I often enjoyed it, especially toasted in the grate of the stove or on the top of the camp cooking stove in the Speisesaal. Most of us preferred to toast it.

A welcome fatigue was fetching Red Cross parcels from the station — in the same cart used to haul bread. The parcels, really cardboard cartons weighing about eleven pounds, arrived regularly enough for every man to receive one a week during the greater part of the war. They contained well chosen foodstuffs including canned milk or powdered milk, butter, sugar, some kind of meat such as corned beef or spam, coffee, tea or cocoa, biscuits, chocolate, jam or marmalade. We depended on the parcels, could hardly have survived without them, and it would be difficult to over-estimate their value to us. One or two rash characters punched two holes in their cans of sweet milk as soon as they laid hands on them and sucked in the whole can at a sitting. Others prudently rationed themselves until the next parcel arrived.

I was sent to Eisenach to be X-rayed and it was found that I did not have ulcers. Excellent attention was received at this clinic. Eisenach was about forty kilometres from the camp. I visited it again to be examined for glasses. A bearded civilian oculist tried a good many glasses set in slots. In due course the spectacles arrived but I could never get used to wearing them. In the train we passed Warburg, the castle where Luther, according to legend, threw an ink pot at the devil. Other trips were to Obermassfeld hospital to visit an Australian dentist, himself captured in North Africa.

Men recovering from sickness went on a weekly laundry fatigue to Vacha, accompanied by the Sanitäter and the inevitable guard. The laundry was carried in sacks and the men waited in Vacha until the clean laundry brought the week before was ready. The guard sometimes purchased articles in the town, bribed with cigarettes. Often the articles desired were simply not there, but over the years a large quantity of odds and ends was bought. Notebooks and pencils were not difficult to obtain. An old woman did the laundry and we sat in her parlour (her old parrot might utter a word or two), or out in her back garden. I remember fearsome engravings, with explanatory text in old German print, illustrating the fate of those who took the downward path. In the nineteenth century Thüringia must have been full of these grim Protestant warnings. We all enjoyed the feeling of normal life in this house. We felt for an hour like free men.

The trips to Vacha were often by train, a short journey, but we walked the three or four miles at other times, partly across country fields. Any trip was welcome — one saw the outside world and there was always the chance of hearing news. Once we walked to Vacha to have our chests X-rayed in a mobile trailer unit.

At the camp, probably in 1942, a party of German army doctors examined and measured every man's chest for depth. We were glad of these precautions against tuberculosis because the rooms were stuffy at night. Up to twenty men lived in each room ventilated at both ends by windows that opened outwards five or six inches at the most against iron bars. A black-out frame was lowered over the windows until lights out. These frames were hinged above the windows: heavy building paper nailed to a wooden frame.

The doors to every room were padlocked by the guards soon after the afternoon shift returned after eleven o'clock so there was danger from fire. The building was wood, unplastered, the mattresses were filled with straw and men smoked in bed. We decided to use one of the long, heavy benches as a battering ram with ten or more men if a fire broke out. It would take the guards some time to unbar all the doors.

Twice a year every man put in two or three hours after work doing a fatigue that was very much disliked. The cesspool by the lavatories had to be emptied. The lavatories contained two lines of ten sloping seats with a partition between. Excrement was ladled out of a manhole into buckets which were carried to Klotzbach's vegetable garden beyond the camps to the east. Klotzbach attempted to supervise this work, but never without a row. His manner always irritated us: our reaction made him lose his temper. Supervision was better left to the guards. Now and then a farmer came with a long cylindrical metal container on a wagon and syphoned the contents of the cesspool into it. The vegetable garden received the residue.

Once a week the camp marched up to the large bath-house at the mine for a shower. The morning shift went up about 3:30 in the afternoon having first returned to the camp for dinner. We undressed at benches in a large hall. The German miners' clothes hung above us drawn up to the high roof on pulleys and long chains.

Washing was done at the camp at four terrazzo basins with taps that sprayed water all round so that six or seven men could wash at once. The water was cold. There was a stove in the centre of the washroom to prevent pipes freezing, but in the winter ice formed sometimes. Each room had a bucket. The twenty men washed their clothes in it (laundry sent to Vacha was shirts and bedding). The bucket was used as a toilet during the night. It often overflowed, and the wood floor rotted at that end of the room. The bucket was emptied by the man doing room fatigues, and any other chores that came up in the camp by order of the Kommandant. This duty rotated round the room; every man doing fatigues for one week. Another job for the man on fatigue was drawing bread and sausage rations for the room, slicing the bread in the bread slicer in the Speisesaal, and distributing the rations by putting them on the beds.

We arrived at 137 in July 1940, with shaved heads. By September men wanted haircuts and among one hundred men we had one barber, and one or two who fancied they could cut hair. In later years, when cigarettes were plentiful, it became the custom to give cigarettes for a haircut, the number varying according to scarcity at

75

the time. There were always men able to cut hair, although our original barber, Mo (a Jewish lad from London), got transferred to be a barber at an officers' camp.

During five years I managed to go sick for ten days to two weeks every few months. These periods of rest could be quite enjoyable. Towards the end of the war, a separate room near the washroom was set aside as a sick bay in charge of the Sanitätor. The privilege of lying still and unmolested on a hard wooden bunk in the semi-dark while through the window one saw the sun shine outside, the leaves of the trees mingling in the breeze on the crest of the earth bank rising above the camp, was an exquisite pleasure.

I suppose it was late in 1942 when word went round that men who passed a Medical Board would be repatriated sometime in 1943. A number of men at 137 applied to the Board, including myself, through the Sanitätor who submitted a list of names with details of disabilities. Later we went in groups to the Reserve Lazaret at Obermassfeld and stayed two days for examination. British doctors made reports on us, with X-ray photographs when necessary, and recommendations to the Board. My stomach was X-rayed again at this time. I heard of the trick of swallowing silver paper, but in these cases the German doctors had another X-ray taken and the silver paper showed in a different place or not at all. A friend of mine managed to get a plate showing ulcers substituted for his own, and when the time came he passed the Medical Board.

Some time later in 1943 we received word that a Medical Board examination would be held at Mühlhausen. Molsdorf had been vacated as the Zweilager, or transit camp of Stalag IXC. There were usually about 350 men at these camps.

We went by freight car. The journey took 32 hours and was very uncomfortable — men were not encouraged to go before the Medical Board by the Germans.

Several hundred men arrived at Mühlhausen for the Medical Board. We were given two blankets and billeted down in the cellars, normally used as the air raid shelter. There were several alarms during the three or four days we were there, and then we all crowded in with the normal population of the place. The camp had been a

brewery — an old red brick building of several storeys with crenellated towers.

The Medical Board interviewed us one by one; two or three German doctors and two representing the Swiss Commission, a neutral organization that supervised the treatment of allied prisoners of war. When my turn came a German doctor, with my papers and X-ray photograph, told me that my application had been refused. I was not surprised. I asked him for a light worker's card. He seemed surprised but agreed.

I never saw this card. At 137 the Kommandant denied any knowledge of it, but it must have come through, for after some trouble and persistence I got light work at the mine. In one way it became a liability. There was continual pressure on me to do heavy jobs that I had to resist; other men with light workers cards resisted also. These continual rows with the Betriebsführer, Meisters and guards were more troublesome than working on the transport gang. Besides, a shift seemed intolerably long doing these light jobs because they were usually done alone.

A Canadian refused to do his work in the Löserhaus, and his Meister telephoned the camp for two guards to come and make him work. Being nearby, the Canadian (who spoke no German) shouted to me to explain to the guards that he should be doing only light work. By this time one guard was too infuriated to listen. He pushed his rifle-barrel against my chest. I could see his finger fumbling at the trigger and his suffused, yelling face. I ducked down suddenly and got away behind some steel tubs. The Canadian went back to camp under guard.

A little later I was put back on Göbel's gang as a punishment for suspected sabotage in spite of my light worker's ticket. One morning an Upper Silesian Nazi foreman, not connected with Göbel's gang, ordered me to pick up a square metre of steel plate lying in the muddy ground. Of course I refused. After some shouting he ran at me with a raised pick-axe. I got out of his way in time and he suddenly walked away. No doubt he realized he might be punished for attacking me, but I think his resentment grew out of his experiences, during several months of prisoners trying to enforce recognition of light workers' cards.

The journey from Mühlhausen back to the camp took a long time — twice the car was shunted into sidings and left — we thought it had been forgotten. The car roof leaked. There were pools of water on the floor boards so we stood up night and day.

In due course, those who had passed the Board were ordered to pack their kitbags. As usual it was at short notice, a good thing because the joy of those who were going was tempered by embarrassment. The difference between repatriation and staying on at 137 was too profound for expression. They would be home in a few weeks. Those who remained had no idea how much longer they would have to stay, or whether they would ever leave Germany. I forget how many left — perhaps only five or six.

Christmas came five times while I was at 137. It was a very special day, perhaps because most prisoners felt their separation from home and family more than at any other time. Great preparations were made for Christmas dinner and the decoration of the rooms. Every syndicate put aside items from the weekly Red Cross food parcels, and some brought in flour from the mine in sufficient quantities to bake pies and cakes. Cigarettes were exchanged for flour, eggs or sausages brought to the mine for the purpose by German workmen; but coffee and cocoa were also highly valued by German civilians. Food obtained at the mine was constantly smuggled into the camp. Often, all prisoners were searched both before leaving the mine and on arrival at the camp, the men still drawn up on the cinder path. Nevertheless the contraband was seldom found. The camp did not prepare for Christmas as a whole, but every syndicate was responsible for its own Christmas dinner. Syndicates, or combines — some used one word, some the other — had two or more members up to six or seven. Sometimes, it is true, a whole room, in which there were several syndicates, made a large cake, the ingredients contributed by all the syndicates. We were not without several good cooks. Our first Christmas was celebrated before food parcels or cigarettes began to arrive, so no Christmas dinner was possible, but our rations were increased slightly for that day. The Germans, themselves, made considerable preparations for Christmas. The amount and quality of our Christmas dinners thereafter was remarkable and amazed the guards — for instance, the elaborate decoration of cakes and pastry. We considered this good propaganda. Sometimes someone smuggled in a bottle of Schnapps.

A special entertainment, such as a revue, was put on with painted scenery and costumes. One year a large backdrop of the White Cliffs of Dover painted on sheets of building paper joined together, added something to the festivities.

III

We had news of the war. We were better informed, in some ways, than the public in allied countries, except about the war with Japan.

After 1941, first-hand accounts of Africa, Crete, Malta and the Mediterranean were to be heard in hospitals, and from a few men who came to 137. Later it was difficult to keep up with news from arrivals. Thirty Canadians arrived from the Dieppe Raid in 1942 after a period at Molsdorf. The next large influx was of South Africans brought up from Italy in 1943. From the first we had "the sailor" a veteran of Narvik with us.

We had the news as quickly as the German public. Someone during a shift, if not several, got the news in the German papers and the BBC news in German picked up by German workmen on their radios. Now and then a German did not appear at work and we heard that the Gestapo had made a night visit to his house. During our first year the Germans had complete confidence in victory — confidence that thereafter gradually began to leave them.

Among the German workers were anti-Nazis as fanatical as the active Nazi party members. These were the men who traded bread, eggs and sausages for cigarettes and cocoa. I believe the proportion of fanatical Nazis was one-third, anti-Nazis one-third, apparently neutral, one-third. That would place five hundred men in each category.

Many of the apparently neutral were no doubt cautious anti-Nazis.

Poles, quartered in the village, some prisoners of war, some slave workers, gave us news unobtainable otherwise. Some Poles were allowed fourteen days leave annually to return to Poland. They came back — otherwise no others could go. Inevitably much of our news was inaccurate — rumours were always numerous. But it could often be checked and at least we could select probabilities.

Daily, while at work I spent ten or fifteen minutes at the lavatory getting news from men on other gangs, British, Polish or German. A time came when we were restricted to one lavatory with the Poles and Russians. It was dirtier and wetter than ever.

In Berlin the Germans published a newspaper in English for British and Commonwealth prisoners of war. *The Camp* was a propaganda paper (about six pages) distributed free, one to each man, in the camps. It contained war news editorials, articles on all subjects, and photographs. It was read widely in the beginning for something to read. When books arrived, in book parcels to individuals, and in travelling libraries sent from Geneva by the International Red Cross (about one hundred books a month or more to each camp), fewer men read *The Camp*. We scanned it to see what poison it contained until it ceased to arrive about January 1944. *The Camp*, fairly well edited, was ineffective as propaganda at 137. Americans had a paper called *O.K.* and the French had *Trait-d'Union* rather more intellectual, I found, in my attempts to read a few copies.

One Sunday morning the transport gang had to work. Not an unusual occurrence, but we were tired of it. As usual we protested both at the mine and to the Kommandant at the camp. The deputation, of which I made one, told the Kommandant firmly that we would not work (The Geneva Convention allowed a prisoner one day of rest in seven). After some discussion in the Kommandant's office the Kommandant, bored with the affair, picked up a rifle that was leaning against the wall and asked us if the guards would have to use it. There was nothing to be done and the early morning found us bad-tempered and depressed. When we reached the Frühstück room to change, an old Pole sweeping the floor told us Germany had attacked Russia. It was June 22nd, 1941, and the news was vital and gave courage to the most pessimistic among us. Afterwards, for me at least, there was certainty of ultimate victory.

The Nazis at the mine gave the Russian campaign five or six weeks. We were able to remind them of their boasts of Russia's vast power as an ally. We had borne much propaganda about the vast

numbers of Russia's planes and men. After this, "England kaput" was heard much less often. We heard of the entry of the United States into the war with as little delay, about six months later, and news of the Normandy landing immediately it occurred, having expected it for a long time.

We were pushing the railway hand-car loaded with steel rails one morning in the spring of 1941 when a workman came over to tell Göbel that Hess had flown to Scotland. We never solved that puzzle.

In 1941, one Sunday morning, the guard's radio (the guard-room was next door to room five) woke me up. Lord Haw Haw was broadcasting in English and a guard had the volume turned up for us to hear. His description of the German army crossing Mount Olympus into Greece was menacing and exultant. We had to rely on faith and I must say there was no lack of it in those bad times. By October 1942, I could believe that Germany would eventually lose the war. It was Stalingrad time.

My light worker's card got me an easy job on the third floor of the Löserhaus in the summer of 1944. There was a huge circular tank needing occasional attention. Ritz, an old German, was the only other worker on the floor. He sometimes traded bread, sausages and eggs for my cocoa and coffee. He was a safe German, up to that time not a member of the Nazi party although for several months pressure had been put on him in his village. He wore his first world war iron cross ribbon as a defence. He was small, vehement, with a large, wispy moustache. About five one afternoon he returned after a short absence too exasperated to control his feelings.

"That swine Hitler!" he yelled in German. "Der Lumpe!"

"What's the matter?" I asked, used to his complaints, usually uttered in a low voice with an eye for all points of entry. I had never seen him so careless.

"They tried to kill Hitler," he told me, "this afternoon. They exploded a bomb at a meeting when he was present — and then made a mess of it. The damn fools!"

The old man hated the regime. One of his sons, an Unteroffizier, was told that if he gave up his religion (the family was Roman Catholic) he would be promoted to train troops in a garrison town

in Germany. If he preferred to remain Catholic he would go to the Russian front. He chose the Russian front and was killed.

After arrival at 137 we regularly received one letter form and two postcards twice a month. I often found it difficult to fill them, there was so little to say, although I always sent my full quota. But we all looked forward to receiving letters from a world where all kinds of different things happened. Twice we were able to send photographs home. A civilian photographer came to the camp and took each of the five rooms as a group posed outside on the path. The photographs were paid for with *Lagergeld* changed into marks. Photographs and fruit bought in our first autumn, and the camp piano, were ways of spending money earned at the mine. Otherwise the seventy pfennigs a day paid to each worker under the Geneva Convention were worthless. Roughly printed notes of different colours according to their amount were issued about once a month.

News from home in letters was confined to personal matters by the censors, allied and German. There was no limit to the number of letters that could be received. One man's wife wrote every day. Censors cut out words and sentences with scissors, sometimes. Written in red pencil on a letter of mine, that looked like a paper cut-out, was "Don't blame the German censor for this!"

At the old dance hall at Bad Sulza I had made notes unconnected with the war, and I continued to make notes at 137. A guard got me a notebook at Vacha for a few cigarettes. I valued it highly. It was always in danger, particularly from Kontrols but any guard who found it might take it to the Kommandant, so in 1943 I applied to have it censored and stamped at Bad Sulza. There were interpreters there who spoke perfect English. I remember one who, moving off after a conversation said, "Well, see you in church." My notebook was stamped and returned.

At intervals of one to two years a Kontrol descended on the camp. Completely unexpected by prisoners and guards a truck drew up at the camp gates. Half a dozen soldiers under an officer ran down the cinder path shouting "Raus, raus. Los, los!" Our guards took up the cry, ordering all out of the rooms to line up on the path. They tried to catch us unawares before we could think of hiding anything. During one Kontrol we stayed outside for five hours while the soldiers emptied mattresses and pillow cases of straw, emptied the cupboards and searched everywhere. Every man was searched in the Speisesaal. We had to undress; have our boots examined. At 2:00 a.m. when the search ended all our belongings were in heaps in the rooms. The morning shift had to get up at 3:30 a.m. as usual. The major in command shouted and threatened until he was tired out. I lost nothing on these occasions. The Kontrol always missed the things they wanted to find. There were home-made maps, drawn by escapers, that were not discovered, pinned to the underside of lower shelves. Kontrols must have been carried out mainly for their psychological effect.

THE MARCH, 1945

I

By the end of March 1945, the sound of guns to the southwest was loud and continual. A slight noise like a door slammed in the distance had in three weeks become gunfire. Even at the beginning of March a careful listener heard a low grumbling like thunder from Frankfurt-am-Main, and on March 30th an occasional machine-gun burst seemed to bring very near our chance of freedom.

During the night of March 30th, when some of my companions did not undress, there was German military activity on a road visible from the camp windows. There was a bright moon. Staff cars, tanks and armoured vehicles used that road. The continual low thunder of the past few weeks had ceased. There was an intense silence when there were no cars on the road. A plane strafed a road somewhere, and two or three tanks fired rather close to us but the night passed without incident.

The twenty men in room five were up early, and there was the usual confusion as we prepared breakfast. The central stove was piled dangerously with pots and kettles. Red Cross cardboard boxes full of tins were spread all over the table. We did not like it so untidy but we were used to it. Outside was still. The great, steel wheels hung motionless above the shaft of the salt mine. The Volksturm guard walked slowly up and down on the railway bridge. He was a foreman at the mine inordinately proud of an excuse to wear his peaked army cap of the first world war. But his strutting walk had become noticeably less confident.

Everyone had a good breakfast. There was no sense in saving food now. It was a protracted meal interrupted by packing necessities in haversacks and kitbags. A move had been expected for several weeks, because of the proximity of fighting, and now it seemed the time had come to leave Arbeits Kommando 137, for better or worse.

About eleven o'clock a terrific crash shook the room as a shell landed a few hundred yards away. Others followed, the spurting clouds of earth and smoke plainly visible. We hoped they wouldn't shorten the range. An engine ran down the local line and passed over the railway bridge. As it came level with the camp and two hundred yards away, a shell landed beside it without stopping it.

The excited guards decided to abandon the camp or, at least, to take cover in two air raid shelters in a hill rising against one side of the camp. Prisoners were ordered to vacate their rooms and enter the shelters. Some of us, preferring to stay until the Americans arrived, went into two cellars used as potato stores and were prepared to take our chance there, but guards found us. They had rifles and bayonets so we joined the others.

With difficulty, the hundred and twenty or so men and guards crowded into the shelters which penetrated the hillside in a straight line. The Kommandant changed his mind and ordered us out. With much grumbling the camp began to straggle towards some woods to the south. Afterwards I heard that American planes fired straight into the mouth of each shelter and tanks dropped two shells on the buildings of the camp.

We did not stay long in the wood, but pushed on up a hill to a huge, plateau-like ploughed field. We were going to Vacha and shells passed overhead and crashed into the town. A group of us waited near a broken down shack, the only visible habitation, while the larger group caught up. An old couple living there seemed to be extremely primitive, but their seamed toothless faces were not un-kindly. They did not seem particularly concerned. There was talk of overpowering the one guard with us, but there was no cover in the immense expanse of ploughed land, and the other guards, although distant, could see us. So we continued and halted at last at the outskirts of the town of Vacha. The Kommandant decided to stay on a hillside covered with bushes beside the road entering Vacha from the west. It was a cold, rainy day and we expected to spend the night on the hillside. We thought the American tanks would enter the town at this point and clear out the hillside as they came round the bend. On top of the same hill German soldiers were digging gun pits. One of them, a young lad, came down the hill past us to get drinking water. He said he had been with the front line as it retreated from Koblenz, and that he and his companions were preparing to stop the Americans when they came down the road. It was a black prospect for us. So we were relieved when, about six o'clock, the Kommandant decided to proceed and we marched through Vacha. Knowing the town we noticed the shell damage. A hundred or more German front line troops, most of them sixteen or seventeen years old, waited to defend the town. They wore torn, camouflaged water-proof shirts over their uniforms, and cloth caps. Some carried Panzer-fausts on their shoulders (anti-tank weapons, known to our side as Bazookas). They stood on the pavement watching us pass, neither friendly nor unfriendly.

We got on the road that leads to Bad Sulzungen, tired as most of us had heavy greatcoats, and all of us carried kit: extra clothing, perhaps a blanket and as much of the remains of our Red Cross parcels packed into haversacks and kitbags. Some with foresight had made a bag with shoulder straps. Others carried kitbags over one shoulder. But even the best made haversacks pulled on the shoulders and restricted circulation. Nearly everyone had a water bottle — a brown enamelled type sold to us for use at the mine.

When quite dark, about eleven-thirty, we reached a service station and sat or lay down while the Kommandant went to see about billets. After a long argument with a man in charge of a vacated Italian camp we were ordered on. Getting up with difficulty, because we were stiff, we went up a side road to the barbed wire enclosure. In order of arrival about fifteen men were allotted to each room. There were no lights. Match flares showed two tier wooden beds without bedboards but we were glad to lie on the floor.

In the morning the situation seemed better as it became known that we would stay. I moved into another room where the other members of my syndicate had spent the night. Each of us carried provisions belonging to the others.

Someone lit a fire and the round stove top was immediately covered with mess tins and kettles. As men were always cooking the fire was kept on all day, and a pile of long thin pieces of wood to be used to finish the buildings gradually disappeared. Now and then bombs were dropped some distance away and occasionally we heard artillery from the direction of Vacha.

The Man of Confidence arranged the preparation of a stew by asking those who still had any to contribute a tin of meat. He got potatoes locally. As the day ended it seemed possible we could remain the next day. We wanted to stay because the Americans would soon come through. In the direction we would march a red glow showed that the town of Bad Sulzungen was in flames.

We stayed another day, and on the next marched to Bad Sulzungen. Many railway trucks were burnt. An ammunition train had drawn in and been bombed. The explosion broke most of the windows in the town and destroyed nearby roofs.

Bad Sulzungen pleasantly surprised us. After waiting on the grass of a public park (these periods of waiting formed an important part of our life) we filed up to a warehouse to collect one American Red Cross parcel to be shared between two men. Also we each received six packets of Marvel cigarettes. The Control Officer, Kommandant and guards received a share also which annoyed some of us, but I could see no harm in it in those last days, for the stores would soon be looted whatever happened. It kept them in a better humour, more likely to agree to our requests. We had no time to unpack the parcels and stow them in our haversacks. They were very awkward to carry in addition to our kit.

On leaving Bad Sulzungen we crossed a stone bridge, soldiers standing by waiting to blow it up. We marched northeast along the valley in the direction of Gotha. Ahead of us magnesium operation flares were being dropped by the Americans. We passed one or two companies of *Volkstürme*, the home-guard, going back to the front, if there was a definite front. They were the middle-aged butchers and bakers and candlestick makers of the nearby villages. It seemed a good time to escape and hide in the woods, but half the Red Cross parcel I carried belonged to someone else, not a member of our syndicate, and I had no idea of giving up my share.

About midday the column stopped for a rest in the grounds of a dilapidated brick factory. Russians from Vacha came in while we were there, perhaps three or four score hungry men in rags. Their guards boiled some potatoes unpeeled in a large cauldron.

Suddenly we saw about a hundred British prisoners approaching by another road. They came from Oechsenburg. The two camps went on in one column. We had all begun to feel weary. As we approached some scattered houses and a garage, rain fell heavily and we waited, trying to shelter under the eaves, while the Kommandant limped off to look for a billet. It was fortunate he was lame and used a stick, for he was anxious to rest occasionally. This time he failed to find a billet and we set out again in the dusk. We went northeast but our ultimate destination was unknown. Some thought we would go north to Mühlhausen, the main camp of the Stalag, and wait there until the Americans took the town. Perhaps the Control Officer who had joined the column took orders from day to day by telephone. He rode a bicycle, but the Kommandant, an Oberfeldwebel, the highest non-commissioned rank, limped along with his stick.

Our guards were, with one or two exceptions, remarkably good from our point of view. At the time of the March a Dienst guard called Charlie had been with us a long time. Charlie was popular. Unlike most guards he was young, but he had lost one eye and had been otherwise wounded on the Russian front. Guards who had been front line soldiers treated us with more understanding than the others.

At this time we had with us an Upper Silesian Pole who had been forced into the German army. He had been in charge of the Alsatian watchdog, but was a friendly anti-Nazi. A carpenter's workshop in one of the villages we passed through belonged to him, and after setting out again that fourth evening he suggested using his workshop as a billet for the night. We reached the village about nine and waited a long time in the main street, but the workshop being considered unsuitable by the Kommandant, we marched on passing picturesque stone buildings seeming, in the moonlight, to grow out of precipitous crags. At midnight we reached a large barn with hay piled twenty or thirty feet high, where the two hundred men were to spend the night. The head of the column got the best places, but there was enough room for everyone to lie down. We were tired.

93

However, it was two hours before the barn was quiet. Men had places high up on top of the hay and others without hay to lie on began undermining the high places, taking no notice of the arguments and threats of those on top. The parcels were divided and packed away. After a meal we wanted to smoke but the danger from fire was so great that the farmer threatened to turn us all out if he saw a lighted cigarette.

I have slept in barns many times with the army in France and on the second march as a prisoner of war, but I have never known the no smoking order to be obeyed, no matter what punishment was threatened. In the next few weeks we often spent the night on deep piles of dry hay. If a fire had started very few could have escaped, perhaps none, because the way out was usually a small door leading to a ladder or narrow stairs.

In the darkness we had thought the barn was isolated, but morning revealed a small village. Friendly people exchanged cigarettes and cocoa for bread. Prisoners entered the houses and often returned with a bulge in their battle dress jackets made by a loaf of bread. I washed and shaved at a tap in a steamy cow-byre.

We left one man behind when we marched away. He was too lame to walk and was prepared to take his chance. The Kommandant allowed him to stay because there was no way of taking him with us. No doubt he was freed by the Americans a few days later.

II

We entered a region of fir and pine trees — the Thüringian Forest. The forest is about eighty miles long; in the shape of a cigar from northwest to southeast. Marching became more interesting in this region of hills and small mountains, but its winding and hilly roads increased our marching distance. Tall evergreen trees stood at each side of the road, the branches meeting far overhead. American planes circled looking for movement on the road. In open country we might be distinguished from the air as prisoners of war, but marching along narrow forest roads we were in constant danger of being machine-gunned. At this time there were no German planes over Thüringia. The Americans had the air to themselves and one or two droned overhead all day. In France in 1940 we seldom saw a French or British plane, and were in constant trouble from hedge-hopping German planes which seemed to be everywhere. Now allied airmen had to be watched. If one had turned over and dived on us only those quick enough to throw themselves off the road might have escaped. Now and then a plane dived behind us or in front of us when a German tank ventured along the road. We frequently passed tanks in the trees. Their crews made it impractical to escape and hide in the forest, for we would be certain to be seen by them, or by anti-aircraft units hidden in the trees. I believe now that there was a good chance of surviving after being seen by German troops, but at the time we thought they would shoot us. While still in the camp, as the sound of guns became louder and louder some believed that German front line troops falling back past prison camps would turn machine guns on them. I have never heard that this happened.

We still marched east and southeast. By afternoon we passed a narrow gorge between high rock walls. Streams splashed over rocky ledges into pools. Rustic seats near the waterfalls showed that the place was a resort. It was a dangerous road for American tanks for tank traps had increased its natural defensive strength. Timber of nine inches to a foot in diameter made a trap when placed between the many posts driven into the ground beside the road. Groups of Volkstürme stood by waiting to complete the traps. The beauty of the spring day was spoiled as if it had taken on some kind of tarnish, or turned sour or acrid. When we rested beside the road my trembling thighs were almost paralysed with fatigue. Then the great column began to move, and I stood up with enormous effort.

Since leaving the camp the sound of guns had varied from near to far. Sometimes German artillery fired from a hidden position nearby, and sometimes an American shell crashed in the forest. The Americans advanced at the rate we marched because we could always hear the front line at certain times of the day and night, but there were long periods of absolute quiet.

We reached an understanding with the Kommandant to halt and sit beside the road ten minutes in every hour. The Kommandant's lameness and the age of two of our guards, game old fellows, veterans of the first world war, helped us. The old guards were popular. At resting time we removed our packs and sat or lay down. Pack straps prevented proper circulation, and there was a strain on the shoulders. We needed water bottles, but they hung from our shoulders and added to our aches and pains. It was a great pleasure to lie at full length and smoke a cigarette. The sombre forest rose on all sides, straight and silent.

A large vacant school in Zella sheltered us for the night. The town buzzed with rumours. We could not leave the school but talked to civilians from some of the back windows. They said Americans were expected during the night and that white flags were being hung out. Some of us had offers of help from civilians and, encouraged by the rumours, two or three escaped during the night. As usual the rumours were false. Someone saw some white towels hanging up to dry, but some excitement was caused and we hoped the tanks would enter the town during the night.

Soon after we had selected a place on the stone floor our Man of Confidence asked everyone to report sick in an attempt to compel the guards to leave us in the school. He wanted co-operation from the other camp marching with us. It was refused and the manoeuvre failed. The Control Officer went to see a German army doctor and returned after hearing threats of severe disciplinary action. The Sanitätor of our camp had many dressings to make as by now about thirty men had blistered feet and his supply of disinfectant and bandages ran short.

We received some potatoes boiled in their skins and hot water to which we added cocoa or coffee. Most of us still had food and cigarettes. We hoped to be awakened by American tanks, but in the morning the situation was unaltered. As we marched out of Zella we saw no white flags.

The road wound through the forest between the conical Thüringian hills. American planes gave us some nervous moments. We saw them dive on the road ahead, and a few minutes later we found a pool of blood and a pair of smashed goggles, or a tank, its steel plates unbelievably riddled and twisted. It always worried us when a German tank parked where we rested, or when a company of soldiers passed us, or worse, rested beside us. We then became a target.

We saw rifles and sub-machine guns thrown under the trees beside the road by deserting troops and Volkstürme. Even S.S. troops were deserting and hiding in the forest or in houses. Our continual refrain, particularly while resting beside the road was "why don't the silly bastards pack in?"

III

We reached a village in the evening where there was difficulty in finding a billet, but in the end the upper floor of an empty two-storey building was allotted to us. For some unknown reason we had remarkable freedom in this village, although a long German convoy of tanks and *Wehrmacht* trucks passed through it before dark. By passing through one or two farmyards it was possible to reach a stream for a wash, and to trade with the inhabitants if one could spare cigarettes, soap or cocoa. The people talked freely. All of us spoke some German, however badly, and some of us spoke it well.

The room, at the top of a narrow flight of steps, had to hold two hundred men and it was difficult to get a space large enough to lie down. One of a syndicate arriving first reserved a space for his friends, so that those coming in last often had bad positions and too little room. During this March, as during the first in 1940, every man cared only for himself and his syndicate. Others received no consideration. There were exceptions, notably the behaviour of the Man of Confidence in charge of all men from my camp. He did his job notably well, without favour and without fear of the Germans.

The weight of packs was a problem. No one liked to throw away useful articles and very few carried anything useless, although one man from Oechsenburg still carried a big mandolin, and another had a large photograph, complete with frame and glass. Food was essential. Most Red Cross food was canned and heavy. Things not badly needed were being left behind, but a few carried kitbags on a shoulder without any straps, or heavy suitcases as if they were on a railway platform.

The following day was one of the worst and most tiring days of the March. We had been close to the shifting line between the retreating and advancing armies all the way, and periodically hoped we were cut off by a pincer movement and could not be forced to march further. All this was supposition. On this day I think we may have been nearly cut off, but the local general instructed the Control Officer and Kommandant to get us through the gap. At times we approached to within two miles of fighting, and I have no doubt were once or twice on the front line if such a line could be said to exist. Dodging prisoners of war through the front line is against all the rules, and the Germans should have let us stay in some town or village until it fell. But it seemed to be the policy of German military commanders to prevent us being freed, although we could not think of a good reason why they should at that stage. Now, I believe an order affecting all prisoners came from very high up, possibly from the insane Himmler. The Americans would have sent us to the rear.

We halted at noon and withdrew from the road into the trees. The Kommandant thought we would stay there for the night. After a two hour wait, however, he decided to go on and we continued the March after some argument and protests. Soon we reached much flatter country. We had come out on the east side of the forest and were on a paved road. Beside it, in a ditch, lay bodies of Russian prisoners in German uniforms of the 1914-18 war with S.U. painted on their backs. Their bare, yellow feet stuck up at odd angles. Further on were German tanks, the crews standing ready to take them into action. On the west side was the forest and to the east flat, peaceful country stretched into the distance. A farm girl wobbled past on a bicycle as if it were a Sunday afternoon in peacetime and, here and there, a peasant worked in a field. It was quiet and ominous. I felt that the bright, calm afternoon was false; that it was somehow darkening. At our next resting place an officer drew his pistol on one or two of our boys who penetrated a little into the trees to relieve themselves, as there were civilians on the road. Luckily one of the guards persuaded him to leave them alone.

We marched into the town of Crawinkel to stay for the night, and stood about in the main street while the Kommandant found shelter. Quite unexpectedly, out of the blue sky, a shell burst in our part of the street. We got our heads down but there was no shelter. Several shells burst at intervals of a few seconds. No one was hurt, although I don't know how two hundred or more men escaped. We lost no time in doubling down a side street in the direction of the billet. It was a large camouflaged garage or hangar; the sort of place likely to be bombed or shelled. But everyone was so tired and hungry after a long day's march that it was a relief to stop anywhere. There was a water-tap nearby and we began to light fires beside the hangar regardless of the danger of drawing attention to the place. As it was getting dark a shell whistled overhead and fell in front of the hangar, and although very weary we should all have preferred to march out of that town.

The cold night began quietly. Some men, because of the nearness of the Americans, did not take off their boots. Four escaped in the dark and hid in a small wooden shed about three hundred yards away. After the war I heard from one of them that they were discovered by the Bürgermeister after the rest of us had left, and that he brought a couple of soldiers. The soldiers were friendly and allowed them to stay until the Americans entered the town.

About midnight, German artillery began firing from some trees a quarter of a mile to one side of us and those who had removed their boots put them on. We all arranged our kit in the dark for the Americans might reply, and we were far too near the German gun. Before dawn a shell seemed to slither along the roof of the hangar and crashed in front. For half an hour or longer shells came over, every one seeming to touch the long hangar roof and falling nearer and nearer the front of the building.

Shortly after dawn the Kommandant decided to evacuate the hangar and we left Crawinkel. We marched heavily across rain-soaked fields into hilly country. Mounting higher we reached a village about noon and retired off the road to the shelter of a forest for a two or three hour rest and a meal made up of what we had left of the Red Cross parcels. We had come a considerable distance from Crawinkel and the village and woods were peaceful. The guards were lax, and men began gradually to get away under cover of fences and trees and knock on the doors of houses. They offered to buy food or hot water to make cocoa. Later an arrangement was made at a house for hot water for all of us. The water was boiled in a large copper boiler in a barn, but long before it was ready some of those who had "tapped" houses for hot water returned with it or with loaves of

bread under their jackets. The people were remarkably friendly. Anyone who asked at enough houses got something to eat or drink. George, one of the five members of my syndicate, began a successful and adventurous career of "tapping" local inhabitants for food. Even at Crawinkel he had knocked at the Station Master's door and come away with something. When someone answered the door he offered to buy bread, bacon or eggs, perhaps holding mark notes in his hand or a shirt or gloves for exchange. This was officially strictly forbidden, but the practice increased as time passed until, towards the end of the March, everyone had become more or less expert. It was the heyday of the professional door-to-door canvasser and some, like George, had unsuspected talent. He was the star performer of our syndicate. On this day he approached a house where an old lady seemed glad to see him and offered to hide him in the house until the Americans came. He said there were five of us. She suggested that we hide in the woods until nightfall and then come to her house. She took George upstairs to meet "the Greek." They entered an empty room. The old lady opened a wardrobe door and revealed the Greek standing in it. They were introduced and shook hands, the Greek remaining in the wardrobe. Besides the Greek the old lady was hiding five S.S. deserters in her cellar. George favoured this proposition but a majority of the syndicate turned it down. Some of us were wary of the S.S.

Meanwhile several men decided to escape and hide in the forest. The trees were rather far apart but high, so that very little sunlight reached the fir-needle covered forest floor. It undulated enough to give good cover. One at a time the escapers edged further into the trees taking advantage of the dips in the ground and disappeared. I believe ten left us at this village.

Late in the afternoon we came to the large town of Ilmenau. We stopped at a porcelain factory as rain began to fall. The manager of the factory would not allow us to occupy the vacated French prisoners' quarters behind the offices, so we went to another building on the other side of the town. Marching through the main streets we saw dense crowds of people standing in the rain in front of the larger shops and department stores. They waited for the goods to be handed out to them. This was better than a sale and they prevented, by this means, stores of food and clothing from falling into the hands of the American Army. By the railway old women collected coal in barrows. Everything was free. The population did not know when they could get shoes, clothing and coal again. After a long wait on the other side of Ilmenau during which we got wet through, it was found that the billets were not suitable so we returned to the porcelain factory. Rain shone on the black, cobbled streets and the silent crowds, bigger now, waited. Standing in the rain at the porcelain factory put everyone in a savage temper. Our discontent was audible and may have caused the manager to give way because we were eventually allowed to occupy the former French prisoners' barrack rooms. They were dirty and stank and were full of rubbish, but there were stoves in the centre of the rooms and we dried our clothes by burning enough rubbish to make them red hot. We hung clothes and blankets on lines. Pots of water and food were piled precariously on circular stove tops; an unbelievable amount of cooking, as usual, being done on one small stove. It was hard to find enough room to lie down; there was not a square foot uncovered by sleeping men.

In the morning we continued in an east-southeasterly direction, halting at noon in the grounds of an hotel long enough for those with food to eat, and boil water. Some French and Belgian prisoners joined us and added to the many current rumours by saying that Saalfeld had been declared an open town, and that we were all going to stay there until the end of the war. Large numbers of Allied prisoners already lived there, they said. An agreement not to bomb the town had been obtained. The rumour was shown to be false when, some time later, Saalfeld was heavily bombed. We often heard of places that had been declared open towns. Often they were towns we expected to enter in a day or two. We never found one that was open.

We slept on the crowded floor of a prisoner-of-war barracks lately vacated by Italians. There was a cook-house and badly needed potatoes were bought and boiled in their skins. A few Ukrainian slave workers helped in the kitchen, some of them young girls. During the night to go to the door to make water was impossible without treading on men packed on the floor, and there was a possibility of being shot by the local Volkstürme who were over-zealous and guarded the one-storey barracks all night with rifles to prevent us from escaping. Fortunately such over-conscientious Volkstürme were rare.

We were now well away from the forest following the Saale valley towards the east. The outskirts of Rudolstadt were reached at noon on the next day. It was much the largest town we had been through, a long narrow straggling place that had been Schillers birthplace. As we reached a line of large factories air raid sirens wailed all along the valley, one after the other. The column sat down on the grass verge of the road. Nothing happened. Three or four days later the valley was heavily bombed. Clouds of smoke and dust rose high enough to be seen where we were marching far to the southeast. Miles away the sustained thunder of bombing was impressive.

In Rudolstadt naval officers walked about the streets. Of course the town is hundreds of miles from the sea. We thought they might be engaged in the production of a new weapon.

The Control Officer and Kommandant got loaves from an army bakery, and canned meat, liquid cheese in tubs, margarine and sugar from an army food store. Rudolstadt was a garrison town, with large barracks overlooking it from the east, and there was no lack of food. We grumbled about the short rations on which we had to march. The half Red Cross parcel received a week before had been eaten and, as an occasional half dozen potatoes was all the Germans had given us during that week, the food situation was serious. At Rudolstadt every man got a loaf of heavy, greyish army bread, cheese in a tube that could be pressed out like toothpaste, a fifth of a can of meat and some margarine and sugar. It was the ration for a week with potatoes obtained locally when possible. A party pulling a cart fetched food from the army depository and another went for bread while the rest lay in the hot sun watching foreign workers, mostly Italian, taking a Sunday afternoon stroll beside the immensely long wall of the factory where they worked.

A horse and wagon was hired to carry the supplies which, except for the bread, had not yet been issued, and we marched on to the east. Night was falling as we climbed a steep curving road to a barn in the grounds of a castle owned by a professor of Jena University.

It was a pleasant and beautiful place. The grounds were partly wooded and partly laid out in vegetable and flower gardens. An old castle remained in ruins, and a new castle had been built in the nineteenth century near the commanding site of the old one. The castle was the professor's residence. A few officers were quartered there, and a few wealthy and elderly German evacuees. The professor spoke a little English and seemed friendly as he chatted to some of us on his periodical visits to the vegetable garden. He hoped the Americans would not come by that route.

We stayed in these grounds all the next day. I suggested to the syndicate that we hide in the great piles of hay in the barn when the others left. I felt sure the Americans would occupy the place in two or three days and we had enough food to last a week on short rations. However, a majority voted against leaving the column at that place.

There was a local railway line running up the valley at the foot of the steep hill commanded by the castle. A plane appeared suddenly as an ammunition train reached the foot of the hill, swooped on it and destroyed it. After large explosions the small arms ammunition popped for a long time. Several planes took an interest in the castle during the afternoon. As we had taken the opportunity to wash towels and clothes at the pump and spread them on the grass and fences to dry we might have appeared from the air like a German company billeted in the barn but nothing happened. Except for planes the day was quiet. The front was quiet or had moved farther away, and the professor and his gardeners seeded the garden and worked in the greenhouses.

I sat on a garden seat by a white plaster wall, drowsy in the sun, too drowsy to read the copy of *Moll Flanders* which was being destroyed page by page to reduce the weight. Bees blundered and buzzed about the wall. I could see the gardeners through the glass of the potting sheds and the half-timbered barn looked like a barn in England.

Early in the morning we struck south-southeast towards Bavaria taking, at first, a several mile long shortcut through woods. We had quite changed our direction, for to continue east was to meet the

Russian advance. Most of the north had fallen and what remained was about to fall. We had been in Thüringia and going east had completed the horizontal stroke of the letter L. Now we took the direction of the long vertical stroke southward. Thüringia was considered a Nazi stronghold so we looked forward to Catholic Bavaria whose inhabitants were never strong supporters of the Party. I had an idea, also, that further south we would find warmer weather and a more advanced spring. I could never keep warm at night except in a barn full of hay piled on top of me. In the daytime we were often far too hot. We marched in our army greatcoats because we needed them at night.

The next ten days were rather similar and difficult to distinguish. We entered Upper Franconia, a part of Bavaria. The Thüringian lion gave place to the Bavarian crown on signs in the towns. Shrines with glass-enclosured figures of the Virgin were built into the corners of houses or beside the road, and we often passed large, painted crucifixes of iron and wood. In a few days we reached the vicinity of Hof. Strong rumours circulated that there were Red Cross parcels at Hof but, even if there were, we arrived too late. The Germans were preparing to defend it and artillery fire was continuous. We marched until after midnight. For four or five hours after dark we were on the same road as a very long German convoy retreating to the south. Dozens of trucks, charcoal-fuelled, got stuck beside the road causing confusion. As sections of the convoy passed us in the dark on that narrow road, we were crowded up rough grass banks at the side, or into ditches. Rough marching made our packs intolerably heavy. About eleven p.m. we struck across fields and took a deeply rutted, muddy lane to a farm a few miles from Hof. I lost my water bottle in the scramble and consoled myself with the thought of its weight.

We slept in the upper part of one of those great Bavarian barns we were to know so well, and early in the morning made a fire in the yard and began to cook a few stolen potatoes and some dried vegetables bought from a French prisoner. We only had time to half-cook our concoction. The commander of a company of soldiers in the village ordered our Kommandant to get us out of that region before the battle. We were still eating as we formed up for the March.

When we reached Rehau I thought the planes circling overhead looked dangerous and I expected bombers that evening. At six o'clock we stopped at the market square and lay down for a rest. American planes continued to circle overhead and the town was preparing for occupation. The people were willing to let the Americans enter, but between them and the Americans were German front line troops who might fall back on the town and defend it. In Rehau I saw Jews drawn up in a military formation. They wore blue and white striped prison garments with blankets knotted over their heads as a protection against the drizzling rain. They were miserable and desperate. Guards were taking them somewhere from a concentration camp.

We passed within five miles of the Czechoslovakian border and through the edges of the Bohemian forest. Here, there were few towns or farms. The region seemed nearly uninhabited. But American planes kept a sharp look-out for convoys on the road and often came down to machine gun transport or drop a few light bombs.

A region of hills with steep winding roads, half farmland, half irregular forest took several days to cross. Stone castles built high up on crags and precipitous rocks had long ago commanded the forests and farms — now they seemed deserted, a few rooks circling near the conical roofs. This quiet part of Bavaria, were it allowed to, would fall back into contentment and country peace. Its white, winding roads and dark patches of forest look like illustrations of a fairy tale. Old crones carrying faggots, and the ox-drawn carts seemed medieval, yet brightly coloured and cheerful, and one thought again of old myths and tales.

As the column climbed a hill out of a picturesque village built in a hollow, a plane dropped four bombs among the houses; there were German army vehicles hidden in the barns. Large Bavarian barns gave good cover to transport. Built round a courtyard any farm could hide trucks and artillery, and the forest which lined the roads in so many places gave cover to transport driven a few yards under the trees. Women travelled with the drivers and gun crews, some in uniform. We were surprised to see so many women and girls attached to army convoys. Now and then artillery fired from positions in the trees a few yards off the road, boxes of gleaming shells stacked nearby.

V

I shall end the account of this part of the March with a description of a typical day, from waking in the morning to falling asleep at night.

We slept in a barn. Having been awakened in the night by the cold, unless deep in hay, we got up about six, already partly dressed. If wet on arrival the night before our boots would be full of straw which helped to dry them. After a long march in the rain our battle dress was still wet in the morning. Straw had to be picked carefully out of our socks to avoid blisters and sore feet. We washed at a tap, if there was one, or at a pond. Often there was a tap in the cow-byre where the steamy atmosphere was comfortably warm. Most men shaved every other day — a practice I followed.

By now most of us had used up our Red Cross coffee and cocoa. Much of the cocoa had been exchanged for bread. Some had acquired packets of German ersatz coffee, or packets of camomile tea (a tea made of herbs compressed in green cubes) and they tried to get hot water from the farmer. The camomile tea became a substitute for tobacco. Nothing to smoke was felt to be nearly as bad as nothing to eat. There was always a strong rumour that we were approaching a town with Red Cross parcels and cigarettes but on reaching it the parcels were said to be somewhere farther on. The syndicate still had cocoa mixed with powdered milk and sugar in a small cloth bag, so we had cocoa for breakfast when there was time to heat water. This bag of cocoa had been specially saved and prepared before the March began. Breakfast was anything that could be scrounged. We lived on the country for the guards provided nothing for breakfast. Anyone with initiative (there were many) got up early to "tap" local inhabitants for bread, eggs and fat. Sometimes a French prisoner still lived at a nearby farm, and he gave cigarettes and odds and ends of food to the first British prisoner to find him.

Generally, just as those who had provided breakfast for themselves were eating it, the Kommandant came (he had slept in the farm-house) and the guards began to put on their red cowskin covered packs. Our Confidence Man gave us the word and we lined up in threes for the day's march. The Kommandant negotiated for a wagon to carry some of the kit and, if he got one, about a third of the haversacks and kitbags were piled up on it. The wagon was hired to carry the baggage of sick men and men with bad feet but sometimes we all managed to get our heavy packs loaded. It made a great difference to the day.

A ten minute rest came after marching an hour and this alternation continued throughout the day. Only at night, when we had not yet found a billet, we marched for several hours without rest. Rests were welcome, there was often an outcry if they were delayed, but it was hard to get up afterwards and shoulder our packs when we had to carry them. Stiffness had set in, and it took ten minutes to get used to marching again. I often smoked a cigarette when we rested. At first real cigarettes, then cigarettes rolled from carefully preserved dog-ends, then very thin, wispy cigarettes rolled from what we called pocket linings; remnants of tobacco dust found in pockets. At the time of which I write we smoked pocket linings.

One evening the whole column refused to get up after one of these rests unless the Germans gave us food. It was on the outskirts of a factory town passed through without finding a billet. The prospect of an indefinite night march after a long day had put all of us in a bad temper. After half-an-hour of shouting and threatening the Germans made a definite promise to get rations, which no one believed but as it was impossible for them to give us food where we were, we continued to march.

A dangerous trick of the German troops was to attach themselves to our column while planes were overhead searching for them. Once, a company of soldiers — boys fifteen to sixteen years of age — tried to march single file beside our column. They were frightened of a plane overhead. So were we, but they thought they would be safe with us. The column stopped and stood until the field-gray uniformed troops disengaged themselves and took their chance ahead. But khaki was not proof against air attack because Hungarian troops, numerous in Bavaria at this time, wore khaki. Hundreds of British prisoners were killed by allied planes. Our column was never attacked, although on the road for six weeks near battle areas, and although German units on the same road were sometimes destroyed. Perhaps pilots recognized us.

108

We were marching south, into the sun when it was not cloudy or when our greatest enemy, the rain, was not falling, and when the sun had set many of the men began to work forward in the column to claim a space for their syndicates when we reached the barn chosen as a billet. Most syndicates gave one man the job of being first to select a good position. For this reason the pace usually increased so that, at the end of the day when we were most tired, the column did four miles an hour.

At last we reached the farm and halted. After some delay the farmer was found and we streamed towards the entrance of the narrow stairs of the barn. As it was important to get in first, crushing and crowding was usual and our packs blocked the way. The first man of a syndicate decided quickly which piece of unoccupied floor was the best, and he threw down his pack and greatcoat to reserve space. No time was wasted when the syndicate arrived. If not too late at night one or two syndicate members disappeared in search of food, attempting to buy or scrounge some at houses and farms if it were possible by any means to leave the farmyard. Meanwhile, the rest of the syndicate found two or three bricks and firewood and began to cook in the yard. Queer dishes were prepared. Roasted grain was a fashionable meal when the farmer's sacks of wheat were found. There was always a row with the farmer about stolen eggs — they had to be boiled and eaten quickly — or when one or two hens disappeared. Sometimes eggs under sitting hens vanished, a theft which never failed to enrage the farmer and the guards. It was looked upon as the worst of crimes.

Usually the Man of Confidence and the Kommandant bought enough potatoes from the farmer to make a boiling large enough for every man to have four or five. Volunteers filled the big copper boiler found at every farmhouse with water, and the potatoes were boiled in their skins. Potatoes kept us alive. Sometimes a woman of the household would, with great secrecy, give some of us an egg or a piece of bread. One had to be observant not to miss these chances.

It was the best part of the day. With a night's rest before us we ate potatoes and, if there had been good hunting, a more varied meal. We relaxed and discussed the latest rumours and theories of the war.

Preparation for the night was a matter of piling up enough hay to keep warm. Even with plenty of hay it was cold.

VI

We were in the eastern part of Bavaria called Upper Palatinate when, one afternoon, in a forest of fir trees we passed the dead bodies of fifteen Russian prisoners aged seventeen or eighteen. They sprawled face downwards beside the road in field gray German uniforms of the 1918 pattern with the painted letters S.U. on their backs.

Shortly afterwards we entered Tanna and stayed the night in the upstairs dance-hall of a small hotel. Straw lay on the floor and paintings of fat and dubious women dressed as shepherdesses covered the walls. Ornate brackets had once lit the room. Its luxury was not appreciated and we preferred the customary barn, for here fires were out of the question and the townspeople were inaccessible. However, it was not long before someone found his way through some outhouses and sheds and over a brick wall to a potato store. Before night fell it was empty and several of us had narrowly escaped being seen. George got a supply of potatoes for our syndicate. We always took potatoes when we found any and carried them with us. They were heavy, but no man refused to carry food.

We stayed in the dance-hall until the afternoon of the next day. At last the Kommandant had found rations, and Bill from our syndicate went to help fetch them. Bill always had a deal on hand and often managed on such occasions to exchange something for food. He found that the Germans wanted "glamour shirts" (shirts with pointed collars attached) above everything, especially the soldiers, but they were articles we did not have. The rations were honey and bread. Later in the day we received round loaves of dark bread at a Gasthaus about two miles from Tanna.

Before we left Tanna we were joined by another column of British prisoners, and we all continued together. The new lads carried a white towel tied to a stick to be waved when a plane appeared. At other times the guards insisted that it be kept out of sight.

We still marched south and the sound of artillery was never far away, but near Weiden we found a group of farmhouses in peaceful country and stayed there a night and day without hearing any artillery or tank warfare. At last tank guns opened up not far to the north and we knew we would move during the night, or early in the morning.

The farmhouse and buildings were built in the customary style on three sides of a large courtyard paved with stones. As usual, an Alsatian pawed and strained at the end of a twelve foot chain. We were allowed the use of a large copper boiler to cook potatoes bought from the farmer. The Bavarian farmers seemed to have plenty of food hidden away from us and, during the course of the war, from government inspectors. Most of them gave up less than the amounts demanded by the government and cleverly hid grain, preserved eggs, pork and cheese. They made their own soap from ashes and fat and had become self-supporting. At this farm a woman gave me two eggs which had to be eaten quickly, for shortly afterwards the farmer said that eggs had been stolen and we expected a search.

At this farm we ground flour from stolen wheat. Upstairs in the barn was an old grinding machine which could be worked by hand. Sentries gave warning if the farmer or guards approached, and the soft, wheezing sound of the mill could be heard throughout the night. Hundreds of flat, round cakes were baked and these, with potatoes, were the diet because there was little trading to be done in this community. At last the farmer discovered the loss of his sacks of wheat, the bags of flour had to be hidden and cake-baking became a hazardous occupation.

Our syndicate found a horse-stall to sleep in. The floor was covered with straw and we made a table by placing an old door on a box. We cooked over small fires between two bricks or stones on the grass behind the farm. Thirty or forty fires were alight all day. Wood was hard to find so the farmer's woodpile got gradually smaller.

The country around the farm was beautiful; a pattern of small woods and hills and distant villages. A pond lay across the road. We washed our shirts in it and the weather was bright enough to dry them.

We found a propaganda leaflet dropped from a plane. It showed a map of the American advance and a description of the campaign in Germany.

A French prisoner appeared. He told us about Red Cross parcels in a town a few miles away, but said there were none for us as there were fourteen thousand civilian internees there. He was not well received and soon went away. We thought he had some job with the Germans.

In the morning of the second day, for the first time, we saw some sixty American prisoners. (Americans we had seen were airmen in the hospitals.) Under guard they passed along the road in front of the farm. They were in bad shape. Many were ill or exhausted and sat in horse-drawn carts, heads hanging forward. Those who marched were ragged, desperate and dejected. They said they had been prisoners for six months. We couldn't see them long enough to hear details of their confinement. Before we began the march I had heard that American starvation cases weighing ninety pounds had reached a British Reserve Lazaret.

Several days later, while at a farm near a main road, hundreds of Commonwealth prisoners passed us. They were in hard physical condition like ourselves with excellent morale. Like us they were hungry. They had received Red Cross parcels three weeks before. An Australian told me he had marched for fifty-eight days from a camp in East Prussia.

It was a farmyard with a large number of buildings and it was possible to get away under their cover. Joe, one of our syndicate, and I decided it was time we made a foray for food, and we started out from the back of the farm buildings towards some roofs showing above a hill about half a mile away. When we reached them we noticed a village some distance beyond and decided to try it. We kept out of sight of a group of soldiers on a road running parallel to the direction in which we had to go and reached the steep, winding village street without being questioned which, as we wore British uniforms, was inevitable if we had met soldiers or Nazi officials. We entered a yard, and Joe going to a house on the left and I to one on the right collected one or two eggs and pieces of bread from friendly housewives. Proceeding deeper into the village we asked a woman

standing in a garden near some hens if she would sell us some eggs. She asked us to wait for a few minutes, and going up the road returned with a well-dressed man in plus-fours. We thought she had brought the *Bürgermeister*. It was useless to try to get away so we waited for them to come up. The man gave us some eggs with care not to be seen from the neighbouring houses.

"When you get back to England," he said in English, "please tell people that there are a few civilized people still in Germany. Unfortunately we have not been able to voice our opinions for several years."

We thought of getting back with what we had, but in a side street we encountered a butcher who took us to his shop. We drank a large stein of beer and bought several pounds of sausage meat and fat for which he allowed us to pay him in marks. Marks at this time were almost valueless. If a German sold anything to advantage it was for cigarettes, coffee or clothing. There was a French prisoner in the shop who appeared to have had a comparatively good time there. It seemed the Nazis were unpopular in this village, a state of affairs not unheard of in Catholic Bavaria. On the other hand the nearness of the American army may have made them anxious to do us a service. But I do not wish to be ungrateful to the housewives, the butcher and the scholarly gentleman in plus-fours.

VII

One night, several days before we crossed the Danube, we marched late and by dusk were still far from our destination. At the main road of a town we stopped to allow a long column to pass by at right angles to us. At first we could not make out who the people were shuffling along, five abreast. The ranks were badly kept and an overpowering smell rose from them. I realized they were civilian prisoners when I noticed their trousers, once striped blue and white, now blue and gray. Many wore gray blankets over their heads as protection against the rain falling lightly but steadily. I was reminded of the group of Jews I had seen two weeks before, because these people wore their blankets in the same way. I thought also of the line of men and women in their own clothes I had seen in 1943 on the

station platform at Erfurt — people arrested by the police or the Gestapo the day before and who waited, under guard, for the train that would take many of them on their last journey — old men, mothers, smartly dressed young women, criminals; for people of every type and class made up the group that took the nine o'clock prison train.

Wearing large, wooden shoes the column did not march, it shuffled slowly, wearily, over the cobblestones, eyes on the road, shoulders bent. The movement of the column had a horrible, staggering, halting rhythm. The column was like a multitude of puppets in ordered movement, but each awkward and badly made. Hardly a word was spoken. At intervals the sickening musty smell enveloped us. That smell I knew well, having encountered it in a rarified form, but never in such intensity. At least two thousand men and boys (boys were few) passed us and at length we continued in the same direction, following them.

The rain ceased and the rising moon, nearly at the full, suddenly revealed the flat countryside. We soon overtook the long column, passed it and were forced to halt while they passed us. This time there was shouting from the S.S. guards who tried to make the column march in some order. In the moonlight we noticed the backs of those not covered with a blanket were painted with the letters KL (*Koncentrationlager*). Here were prisoners evacuated from concentration camps and forced to march in front of the American advance.

Some spoke English. In answer to our shouted questions one replied that he had been in a concentration camp twelve years. That meant he had been imprisoned ever since the Nazis came to power. Another asked us why we looked so down-hearted. But we were not sorry for ourselves but for them. Those moonlit ivory faces expressed courage, fear, ferocity.

Two or three miles further on we passed a great field of short grass, into which the multitude had been driven for the night. They stood in dense groups. The ground was wet after afternoon and evening rain. One group lit brushwood and the glow of the fire and the rising sparks showed the closely packed throng in black silhouette.

Guards stood in a corner of the field with sub-machine guns, among them three young women.

We reached the village where we were to spend the night in a barn. Before reaching it we had to stand at the side of the road again to let another long column of civilian prisoners pass. They were in even worse condition than those we had seen earlier that night.

Yet their guards kept them at a fairly fast pace. At the end of the column were men hardly able to put one foot in front of the other, but who stumbled along making superhuman efforts to keep up for reasons which, during the following few days we were to become fully aware. Many in this column were French some of them wearing berets, many were German. There seemed to be representatives of every occupied country, and some few who spoke English without an accent may have been British or American. Old mess tins were tied to belts, some carried a bottle, some bundles. All had little clothing, most had bare feet in wooden shoes; a few wore boots.

As the last exhausted prisoners struggled by a growl of protest rose from us at their shouting, gesticulating guards. Our own guards hastened to explain that the S.S. would not hesitate to shoot some of us if we gave them provocation. Luckily the column passed without the S.S. taking any notice of us. However, some of our lads very cleverly got one civilian prisoner out of the ranks and hid him. Later they smuggled him into our barn, fed him and, when we departed, left him well hidden with food and water.

At dawn we saw the second column of civilians standing on a hillside where they had passed the night.

That morning George got away and crossed the valley to a house where he sold a shirt and a pair of gloves for twenty eggs. As we boiled them on a fire made on the grass behind the barn a sudden downpour of rain soaked us to the skin. The civilian prisoners still stood on the hillside.

About noon we left that village, the civilian prisoners having gone on before us, but it was not long before we heard rifle shots and we came upon dead bodies in the ditch beside the road.

Prisoners who were too exhausted to keep up with the others, and who fell behind, were shot through the ears by a guard who followed and who held his rifle horizontally in front of him, the weight of the

rifle taken by his arms and the strap pressing against the back of his neck. Often, I saw this guard following the column with a measured tread as we waited beside the road to give the column time to get away. This black uniformed guard, and probably some of the other S.S. guards shot several hundred civilian prisoners on every one of the four days we marched behind them. The black guard, and most of the others looked like ordinary soldiers and passing them on the street one would notice nothing brutal about their faces. There was an exception, however, in one of the women with the guards whose excessively hard face was to be seen about the large truck loaded with the potatoes, mostly rotten, on which the column was fed, and who would look the part of a woman guard in a film about a concentration camp.

There was greater need for hurry, or the patience of the guards had run out, for the number of dead bodies increased day by day until, no longer left in queer attitudes beside the road; yellow feet or an arm sticking up and a triangle of blood from the mouth, they were neatly stacked as wood is stacked; a row at right angles to the one above. A stack was, perhaps, eight bodies high. During these days it rained often, so that we marched, sometimes, through shallow pools of bloodstained rain that formed in the road.

One night, about eleven, we came up to a line of German soldiers stretching to a grove of trees two or three hundred feet from the road. I thought they were passing heavy sacks down the line, but they were depositing dead bodies among the trees. No doubt they had received an order to remove the bodies from the roadside.

It was a depressing period, for apart from our continual contact with civilian prisoners and their vile smell, it was impossible to dry our clothes and boots and we also were travelling at a greater speed. We reached a barn at twelve-thirty a.m. and were marching again by six a.m. in wet clothes and with little to eat. On the other hand we were well off compared to the civilian prisoners. As we passed a field where they had stood for the night their stench seemed still to hang over it. The beaten grass and scraps and shreds of cloth that littered it seemed to me to retain something of that sinister fury which characterized the thousand or so men who had trampled the grass to bare patches in a few hours. The idea was subjective, but men less impressionable than I am felt the terror of those empty fields.

In such circumstances as the concentration camp prisoners found themselves the effort to survive taken to its limits leaves no sympathy for others, except for a friend or two who pay for it by their support. Everyone is an enemy. The hate, fear and fury of the prisoners was turned on each other as much as on the guards. In contrast to this, Commonwealth prisoners of war, and probably those of other nations, living under much better conditions, admittedly, developed a high morale and were always united against the enemy.

We overtook the political prisoners once more before we left them behind to be shot by their guards or freed by the Americans. They had survived for years by endurance, wariness and every kind of stratagem. One of them had called out that they were going to Munich — probably Dachau, but it is certain they never reached it as prisoners, for Munich was about to fall.

One evening, I think it was the twenty-second of April, we were marching in the rain knowing we still had many kilometres to cover that night, when we heard a strange noise like a loud murmur. In ten minutes it had become much louder. We turned a corner and realized that the sound, now a tremendous roar, came from a compact grove of high trees in a large field below the level of the road. The grove began abruptly and seemed impenetrable as if clipped round its edges. We could see no-one and there was no sign of human visitation on the level green field stretching away from the grove on all sides. But up on the road near where we would pass stood the German guards with their rifles and sub-machine guns. I knew then that the great roaring sound was the shouting of hundreds of men who had lost their comrades in the darkness of that sinister wood, and when I knew the cause I could almost separate the names, now and then, in that overpowering medley of sound which yet, at the same time, held a note of fury and of haunting desperation.

We saw nothing through the dusk and slanting rain except the high compact grove of feathery trees isolated in the field, but we knew that the prisoners were milling around inside without any light, shouting for the friend who had, perhaps, been shot during the day's march. In 1940 the French prisoners called to each other for hours after we reached our daily destination, and here the same thing was carried to the extreme. It was analogous to the relation of the slight smell often noticed in quarters that had been occupied by French prisoners of war to the stench of the column of K.L.'s. It was the same smell differing enormously in intensity.

The sinister grove of voices was the last place we came across the political prisoners. Later, when freed, we saw a few ex-prisoners in blue and gray striped trousers wandering along the roads.

VIII

At Falkenstein, a few miles north of the Danube, we had men sick enough to make the Kommandant consider leaving them in a military hospital. The strong protests and arguments of our Man of Confidence and Sanitätor achieved a visit to a medical officer who sent the sick men to a hospital where they could be left when the German army fell back. They considered themselves lucky and were, no doubt, freed some days before the rest of us. We had an idea that we might meet trouble in some small corner of territory surrounded by the allies, where the Germans might make a last stand. As a matter of fact the Germans intended to make a last stand in the "Alpine Redoubt". We were nearing the Austrian Alps and the German convoys were coming with us. We could not march south indefinitely and no other way lay open.

At this time we heard that there was a large concentration of prisoners at Moosburg, south of the Danube. As usual, the rumour was that we would be left at Moosburg until we were released, and it did not fail to rouse hopes of getting food and cigarettes there, for we heard that it contained a large store of Red Cross parcels. These were supposed to have been brought from Switzerland by the famous white trucks which we had never seen. According to the stories, they came loaded with parcels for distribution among the prisoner-of-war columns marching in Bavaria. They were driven by Red Cross personel and allowed by the German authorities to enter Germany.

We had no sooner settled in a barn at Falkenstein than we were turned out, and sent to another a mile and a half away. It was a wet, draughty building with walls full of large cracks. There seemed no chance of getting food until Bill, who had got away for half an hour, arranged a deal with a farmer for two pounds of flour. The town, built of stone on a high hill, would be pleasant in peace time, the violet hills that enclose the valley of the Danube may be seen, and an expanse of wooded country. That night it was full of German troops. Early next morning we were on our way, beginning a forty kilometre march to a village south of the Danube and east of the capital of the Upper Palatinate, the medieval city of Ratisbon. This city is called Regensburg in Germany and it was about to be defended by S.S. troops.

It was still possible to cross the Danube. We reached a ferry operated by an old man who used the strong current and an overhead wire stretched across the river to propel the ferryboat. The boat was attached to the wire and the old man, by skilful handling of a large rudder progressed slowly in the strong current to the opposite bank. The Danube at this point is a dirty gray-brown, very swift, smooth and dangerous. A swimmer would have little chance in it. Two German officers and their car crossed with us, probably the last passengers before the wire was cut. We crossed in two batches as we numbered well over a hundred.

On the south side lay many square miles of uninhabited flats inundated at floodtime, and beyond them the town of Pfatte in Lower Bavaria. The column had spread out in twos and threes along the road because the first ferry-load went on without waiting for the others. This straggling allowed George to enter a house after an old man beckoned from a window. The old man and his wife gave him milk to drink and a bag of very small delicious sausages which were shared with the syndicate; a kind I had never tasted before. The old couple tried to persuade George to stay with them which he would have done had he not been carrying the syndicate's bread, and some other food that we held in reserve. Pfatte was the most generous town we passed through. The people were remarkably open-handed and friendly, and I believe they had never voluntarily given support to the régime. I refer to the working people whose small houses lined the streets and who supplied us with milk and bread. There was an easily noticeable difference between those people who gave food because the Americans were coming and those who wanted to help us. The latter class were fairly numerous throughout the March, but in parts of Bavaria, as at Pfatte, they astonished us.

We still had a long march ahead of us that day before reaching a large barn where, besides ourselves, there were a few of the German Army Service Corps. These soldiers would have exchanged food for clothing had they had enough for themselves. Unfortunately they were on very short rations. While at this barn we heard the heavy gunfire at Regensburg. Regensburg, or Ratisbon, was once a Roman military outpost to prevent the German tribes from penetrating south of the Danube, and Napoleon fought a battle near it in 1809, but the battle in April 1945 must have been the most serious threat to its existence. During the night shells landed near us where German guns were hidden in the woods.

A German general, who had taken over a house nearby as his headquarters, caused as much inconvenience by insisting that we take cover whenever the local air-raid siren began to wail or a plane flew overhead. As this was very often indeed it seriously interfered with our cooking, done in a field dotted with fireplaces made of loose bricks.

Ten of our own group disappeared at this place, finding hiding places in the cellars and outhouses of local farmers. They got away unobserved behind a group of barns and among the trees beside a stream.

It was rumoured that the large N.C.O. camp, C3, formerly situated near Regensburg had moved to within twelve miles of us. As it was believed they had supplies of Red Cross parcels an unsuccessful attempt was made to communicate with them.

The general, who seemed to be concerned about our welfare, took the trouble to get us rations. We received a considerable quantity of sugar and honey as well as the customary potatoes boiled in the farmhouse copper.

We stayed two nights and a day. Two men decided to hide in a heap of straw inside the barn so, after covering them carefully, we left them behind. I have never heard what happened to those who bailed out at this farm. I hope they were not shot by S.S. retreating from Regensburg. Our syndicate tried to go into the roof space above the farmhouse, which could be reached by a covered-over outside staircase, and hide there, but the farmer put a padlock on the door before we could get in.

Next night it was between dusk and nightfall as we approached dim, whitish farmhouses and entered a barn and courtyard to sleep. Camp 152 stopped at another barn. While at these white-washed farmhouses some of us found an S.S. field kitchen. The soldiers encouraged us to take biscuits and cubes of dried vegetables and soup that they couldn't use, and exchanged bread for articles of clothing. Some of us did a thriving trade cutting German soldiers' hair for cigarettes and tobacco. When we left these houses we waited several hours on the road for the other camp. A plane came down to bomb and machine gun a nearby farm.

We continued to march south, passing through Landshut, a large garrison town, at night. We crossed the Isar by a bridge wired ready to be blown, and a day or two later had crossed the Isen. The days and nights were like many we had experienced in other parts of Bavaria. We were now in Upper Bavaria, approaching the Inn river, tributary of the Danube.

The roads were still full of German military transport. Many trucks were converted from gasoline to gas and burnt wood fuel, others stood abandoned beside the road. Some were towed. The column had to leave the road and climb onto a bank or wait in a ditch while the convoys passed, which added greatly to our physical discomfort. Our packs always seemed heavier standing still than when we marched.

My left thigh had given me trouble ever since I lay in wet fields in 1940, and after a month of marching began to be painful at times. I felt nothing for the first few miles, but for the next four or five it was as if hundreds of needles were being driven into it. The feeling then wore off and I could continue without pain. When nearing Kraiburg, at a time when my leg was at its worst, I got a ride on a baggage wagon, but there were so many on it, that, perched in an uncomfortable position on top of a mountain of packs, I was unable to move. In this condition I passed through the hilly town of Kraiburg and over the Inn where there was a large tank trap which, however, did not trouble the American tanks, as one of their crew afterwards told me. By getting a place on the wagon, though the

126

discomfort was worse than marching, I was able to get the syndicate a place to sleep before the main body arrived. This had become a racket; one member of every syndicate tried to get on the wagon by feigning sickness.

While pausing for a rest the next day, French prisoners quartered in rooms over an inn threw cigarettes out of the windows. It caused such a commotion that the guards could not keep us together. Cigarette tobacco and papers could be bought at some of the other inns, which had not been possible before.

This country is thinly populated. The white, plastered farmhouses are far apart. Occasionally there is a view of mountain ranges to the south and southeast; distant blue and white peaks.

Several prisoners gained admittance to a hospital where they were very well treated, as I afterwards heard, and one of them shared a room with a very amiable German colonel. The hospital was in a town waiting to surrender. The sound of guns was close again. Half a mile away machine guns fired from a wood.

We reached a huge barn after crossing muddy fields in the rain, and spent a miserable morning trying to roast stolen potatoes in sputtering, rain-extinguished fires.

At last, after passing through Trostburg, we reached the town of Palling, about fifteen miles from the Salzberger Alps. From the edge of the town looking southeast they rise from green bases and escarpments. They seemed to be just a few hours walk across the level fields.

IX

The first impression of Palling was bad, although no-one in that column should ever forget its name, or even fail to feel a certain affection for it. We found ourselves in a farmyard more miserable and less convenient for cooking, washing and sleeping than most farmyards we had stayed in. The farmer, gaunt and worried, prowled about forbidding the use of this or that, and persuading the Kommandant to prevent us lighting fires in the paddock.

Gradually the horizon widened. For instance, Phil got out in search of food and visited a schoolmaster, at least a mile away, who agreed to let him and the rest of the syndicate hide in a cave in the hillside at the bottom of his garden. He offered to feed us. We were to go after dark so that no-one would see us enter the cave. We agreed to adopt the plan but before night fell our position had altered.

In the meantime the rest of the syndicate was out "tapping" the inhabitants and getting a slice of bread, an egg or a piece of sausage. The people seemed friendly. I had two large bowls of kraut with some Hungarian soldiers at their field kitchen, and tried to interest some German soldiers in a pair of gloves. They wanted them but had nothing to offer in exchange.

On my return I heard the latest rumour that we were to be left in the town and that the guards were leaving. A Ukrainian vendor offered Ukrainian padded waistcoats for marks, and sold all his stock to us.

Then we were moved to the barns and courtyard which the Hungarians had occupied. The troops were moved out. We took over the largest barn and potatoes were bought and put on to boil in their skins as usual. Fires were lit just outside the courtyard at the edge of a pond. They were first of all forbidden, then no more than fifteen were allowed. Finally the guards lost interest. Their authority was waning rapidly.

The rumour that the guards were leaving us persisted and at last became fact. It was one of the very few rumours that turned into fact. Our guards rode away on bicycles. No one seemed excited, but when the local Führer of the Volksturm asked our Confidence Man what to do next a surrealist element seemed to invade the town. He was advised to meet the Americans with white flags some distance up the road. Neither side wanted American shells dropped into Palling to announce the tanks. Whether the Volksturm took the advice I never heard, but white cloth was hung from windows and a white sheet fluttered on the church spire.

At last we were free, if not yet safe. A rumour that the S.S. might take over the town was not taken seriously but there was uncertainty about our immediate future; we did not know how far away the American Seventh Army was. We wandered about the town trying to persuade the proprietors of public houses to sell us cigarettes. We drank beer at all these Gasthaüsen. German soldiers in the pubs did not seem to be worrying and we discussed the situation with them. A Feldwebel stayed on at our farmhouse, gloomily resigned to Gefangenschaft. The farmhouse kitchen was used by anyone brewing tea, though some respect was shown to the furniture and utensils because the people had been helpful when we arrived. Dozens of eggs and food of all kinds began to arrive as one by one men returned with their spoils, results of a few hours "tapping" of the inhibitants who, by now, dared not refuse.

Our syndicate had more space in the hayloft than usual and plenty of hay to pile on top at night. Someone shot a hole in the roof-tiles with a pistol, otherwise no-one seemed excited. Candles appeared stuck on tins or in bottles near piles of hay. Our luck held, there was no fire.

Before falling asleep that night my mind wandered over the six weeks we had just passed through and back over the five years of Gefangenschaft, five years of which I could remember remarkably little because one day had been too like the next and they were telescoped. In 1940 the camp was new, a long one-storey wooden building of five rooms built for German workers — the *Arbeitsdienst*. We left behind us buildings that looked old. The paint had faded from dark green to pale gray. The cinder path had become hard like cement.

I remembered the Pole we called Buster Keaton who was once a higher civil servant in Warsaw. After five years of pick and shovel work on potatoes and turnip soup, and the grim Polish prisoners' dormitory, and six winters working outside without adequate clothing I saw him one day towards the end, unloading a coal wagon. His ragged coat was fixed at the throat with a piece of wire. In a bemused state, as if drunk, he still used his shovel, but he seemed barely conscious of where he was or what he did.

I remembered the white-haired Russian women repairing the railway in Thüringia. I remembered the fascination German troop-trains had for me, the sleeping heads lolling against window-panes lit up by station lights. I had not grown tired of watching things behind the enemy lines.

I knew it was nearly finished, but I had no realization of it. During the night there was machine-gun and artillery fire.

129

X

American tanks came suddenly round a bend in the road about ten in the morning. It was the great moment. They threw us tins of cream. They asked us how long we had been prisoners, how we had been treated, if we had been at Dachau. Many of the Americans were enraged by what they had seen at Dachau, the concentration camp near Munich. I was rather unpleasantly surprised by the brutal attitude of some of the American officers.

German soldiers straggled into the town to give themselves up. They were gathered together under guard in a field behind the pond. All inhabitants of the town were ordered to leave at once — although many old men and women had nowhere to go. We were told repeatedly to take anything we liked. The Americans said, "The town belongs to you, take it apart." I should have taken this to be irresponsible talk if I had not heard a Californian major say it. Some American soldiers wore half a dozen wrist watches up their arms and had pockets full of cigarette lighters. I saw some take rings from German prisoners. Only a few British prisoners took to looting, the riff-raff among us, most of us were averse to it. Of course we all enjoyed plundering Wehrmacht trucks of food, wine and cigarettes.

Two large trucks were parked in front of a Gasthaus and someone soon thought of looking inside. In a few minutes both trucks were full of men tearing at the contents, filling sacks and passing wine, tinned food and large boxes of cigarettes to their friends on the ground. Some cigarette cartons contained a hundred packets of twenty. When we left Palling we could not carry most of this stuff.

The number of German prisoners increased rapidly so that truck loads had to be taken back to Trostburg where they were quartered in the bombed ruins of a large factory. Hundreds went on foot, and I saw a Polish sailor on a horse herding a group of Germans with a huge whip. I did not see him use it for they gave no trouble. Released Poles enjoyed themselves immensely. When the Americans arrived they appeared in carefully pressed uniforms kept for the occasion.

Generally, the Poles had received bad treatment. Many were forced into the German army. We liked the Poles because we knew which side they were on. They had strong nerves and few were collaborators.

The Americans who released us advanced and others arrived. The front line troops had as many German pistols as they wanted and all the released prisoners had one or two. Lugers were most in demand. The second line of Americans wanted pistols so most of us exchanged ours for watches, cameras or field-glasses.

Germany had always been a vast market place for us. A market where money seldom entered into a transaction. Trading was the activity that persisted at all times in all camps large or small. Men were always "going round the rooms" to exchange a packet of prunes or a bar of chocolate. At the mine we obtained bread or so many eggs for a packet of cocoa smuggled out of the camp. We then had to get the bread or the eggs into the camp where we were searched again. Most German workmen took part in the racket while risking severe penalties if caught. Sometimes guards helped, greatly facilitating trade for a few cigarettes and, sometimes, a good Kommandant would feel bread or a load of eggs while swiftly searching a man without showing that he had noticed anything. Now it was all over, but we still traded.

Everywhere in the streets were piles of rifles, cartridges, hand grenades and Panzerfausts. Dozens of deserted trucks stood in the roads, some still full of Wehrmacht supplies and there were cars, civilian and military. Cars were commandeered and six or seven were brought into our farmyard with the idea of driving them to Le Havre. Two started off full of ex-prisoners and their luggage and, reaching Munich, were very naturally turned back by the American army. There was far too much authorized military traffic on the roads. The rest of us drove around Palling and to Trostburg, but one party venturing too far beyond Palling in the wrong direction was shot by S.S. The war was not yet over.

Bill, George and I drove to Trostburg and lost our car while visiting some Americans at their billet. Someone drove off in it as we enjoyed coffee and eggs and bacon in an expensively furnished and spotlessly clean flat that, as army quarters, was rapidly becoming a shambles. I could not see any reason why it was desirable to destroy other peoples' belongings, and it must have been much more comfortable to live in the flat as it was when they took it over. Our American friends did not seem able to see this point. The Krauts didn't deserve any consideration. After much trouble we found our car. It was wanted by the army but, with the usual remarkable consideration of the American army for all our needs and desires, another car was given us in exchange. Petrol was easy to get. Many an abandoned truck was loaded with containers of it.

German troops kept straggling into Palling to give themselves up and drivers brought their trucks. Our former guards appeared with the unpopular control officer. No serious attempt was made to molest them but, while the control officer and others walked to Trostburg it was arranged for Charlie and another postern to get food and cigarettes and go by truck. Charlie was liked because he kept his head instead of shouting. Shouting on the slightest provocation is a habit among German guards.

I saw the German Bürgermeister and one or two other civilians taken out of Palling by car. Everyone said they were being taken outside the town to be shot. They had been denounced by anti-Nazi inhabitants for their crimes while in office, but there had been no time to give them a trial.

The Americans were trying to arrange transport to take us the first part of our journey to England. Half a dozen large troop transport trucks were necessary. We were all impressed by the American Seventh Army, their kindness to us, their organization and the magnificent efficiency of their transport.

Another phase of our lives had abruptly begun. We had no clear idea about it but it glimmered, full of possibilities, in our imaginations. For some of us this new phase would also be bad.

We spent the first night of our journey at Dachau in the quarters of the concentration camp guards. I saw no evidence of the horror of that camp — twelve years of human misery and torture had left no visible mark.

The next day we reached Mannheim and entered the huge transit camp. We had all been astonished by the bomb damage to the larger German cities. Munich had seemed to be one vast wreck with mounds of earth and rubble, fifteen or twenty feet high where side-

walks had been. Streets of façade windows showed the sky. Mannheim was as bad.

XI

At the Mannheim Camp were ex-prisoners of war of several allied
nations. There were Frenchmen, Jugoslavs, soldiers from India, and
Russians.

The food was good; the camp was administered by the American
army and we had American army rations. Every evening there were
movies shown outside on a large screen set up in the huge parade-
ground. It was only here that the Russians were willing to mingle
with the general ex-prisoner population. Even here they sat as far
apart as possible.

Every morning the Russian ex-prisoners drilled and marched with
a sort of goose-step. They looked extremely serious. We found them
objectionable and like fanatical Nazis. We had no parades and lined
up to draw our rations, etc., in a most casual way.

I took a fancy to the Russian berets, blue with a red star, and went
to their quarters to see if I could exchange something for one. No one
would speak to me; my presence embarrassed them.

After three or four days we went by transport plane to Brussels
and next day crowded into the fuselage of bombers and flew to
England.

I should have preferred to travel by truck or train and by ship
across the Channel. Apart from the fact that a plane came down
killing thirty-six ex-prisoners, I needed time to adjust myself to
freedom. For five years I had looked forward to the day of freedom.
But on that day I felt nothing, neither joy or much relief. It was
another day in the wilderness of days.

We had all learned much, perhaps not so much as we would have
learned in five years of normal living, but what we had learned
could not be learned in any other way. Many of us had come to
despise things we had valued before, and had learned to value things
that we had despised or overlooked. It was up to us whether we
lapsed back into the old grooves of hypocrisy, snobbishness and hum-
bug. At least some of us had been freed.